ENDLESS KNOT

ENDLESS KNOT

*A Spiritual Odyssey
Through
Sado-Masochism*

Mathew Styranka

INSOMNIAC PRESS

Copyright © 2001 by Mathew Styranka.

All rights reserved. No part of this publication may be reproduced, stored in a retrieval system or transmitted, in any form or by any means, without the prior written permission of the publisher or, in the case of photocopying or other reprographic copying, a licence from CANCOPY (Canadian Copyright Licensing Agency), 1 Yonge St., Suite 1900, Toronto, Ontario, Canada, M5E 1E5.

Edited by Jan Barbieri
Copy edited by Richard Almonte
Designed by Cara Scime

National Library of Canada Cataloguing in Publication Data

Styranka, Mathew, 1964–
    Endless knot: a spiritual odyssey through sado-masochism

ISBN 1-894663-10-1

1. Styranka, Mathew, 1964– 2. Sadomasochism–Canada–Biography. I. Title.

HQ79.S86 2001   306.77'5'092   C2001-902145-3

The publisher and the author gratefully acknowledges the support of the Canada Council, the Ontario Arts Council and Department of Canadian Heritage through the Book Publishing Industry Development Program.

Printed and bound in Canada

Insomniac Press, 192 Spadina Avenue, Suite 403,
Toronto, Ontario, Canada, M5T 2C2
www.insomniacpress.com

Author's Note

I do not consider myself an authority on human behaviour, fetish, sado-masochism, meditation or Zen. I have lived my dreams, fantasies and life to the fullest, always with a questioning mind, in search of Truth.

In these pages I have recorded as accurately as possible, from my perspective, events I find integral to my story. The names of people have been changed and some descriptions have been altered in the interest of privacy.

Acknowledgments

While my influences are infinite, there are a few people worth mentioning here:

George Giaouris' fetish parties were a ground on which I played. Without them I don't know how I would have expressed or explored my life-long desires.

I had long given up writing *Endless Knot*, and may never have done so had it not been for the subtle encouragement of Liz Lewis, from *Touch* and *Whiplash* magazines.

I am grateful to Mike O'Connor and everyone at Insomniac Press for their hard work, talent, and most of all, for their interest in me and my story. In particular, my editor, Jan Barbieri, offered a unique perspective and skill which allowed me to express myself as best I could.

Bob Howard's depth of introspection and wisdom have been, and continue to be, a great inspiration to me.

Thanks to those I have mentioned above and to all those people who have opened their hearts to me over the years.

I asked a ninety-two year old man, "If there's one thing you've learned, what is it?"

His grizzled face looked thoughtful for a moment, then he said, "That you can't teach people lessons."

The cavernous bar room was dark and cool, each nook and cranny displaying one spotlit piece of s/m equipment or another: a St. Andrew's cross, a blue leather bench, a suspension bar, chains. The DJ cranked Nine Inch Nails, Ministry and other late 80s industrial and alternative rock. It was early but already people were streaming in—doms, subs, gays, TVs— decked out in everything from frilly lingerie to hard-core bondage gear and covered in piercings. There was a strong, positive vibe. The place was heating up.

  I had on tight-fitting leather pants, a pair of vintage, spit-polished RCMP riding boots that I'd dyed black, and a woven-leather collar and leash. I was fit, just under six feet tall with average proportions, sandy-brown hair and green eyes. I've always been somewhat boyish and women seem to like that. Most of all, my foot massages, borne of love and passion, were in demand.

In the vanilla world, my desires had been mostly hidden. Working on Bay Street in downtown Toronto meant that most of my days were spent hiding who I really was, how I really wanted to be. I rarely had an opportunity where I felt comfortable expressing my foot fetish and my submissiveness. I felt like I couldn't talk to the women I met outside the scene. They wanted a more traditional, established man who was devoted to a career and who had a mind for a home and children. Sexually, they weren't into anything that interested me—they just wanted to be fucked, now. But at fetish nights, I could openly express what I wanted and needed without fear of being negatively judged. As a young man with submissive tendencies and a love of pretty feet, I felt boundless there.

The excitement I felt leading up to each fet night was built on years of this frustration. I'd attended dozens of fet parties and each time my heart was in my throat. In those days, before the parties had gone mainstream, there were countless sexy women attending fet nights. I knew that at each function there would be dozens of boot-encased feet for me to ravage.

The thought of worshipping a woman and her feet, and the possibility of connecting with her as my dom, was almost unbearable. Despite my fetish, it was the woman, not her body, that I craved. With hundreds and hundreds of women and their feet under my tongue, I had yet to find my Mistress.

As always, I had arrived early, changed, checked my things and primed up with a tequila or two by the entrance. Here I watched women come in wearing their extraordinary attire: skin-tight PVC, rubber dresses and leather thigh-high boots. Usually, I spotted women I liked and then, throughout the night, circled around them, hunting, like a shark having sensed blood. I teased myself with my approach, imagining a particular woman, what she smelled and tasted like, what her feet looked, smelled and tasted like, how she would react to my worship. I made it last all night, sometimes having up to five different women in one evening. I was desperately oral and consequently submissive. I was a slave to my desires, if not to any Mistress.

I almost missed her and only saw her as she walked away, toward the coat check at the rear of the club. As hot as she looked from my vantage point, I hadn't seen enough of her features to justify the lead ball I felt in the pit of my stomach; what drew me to her was invisible. It was the way she moved, the way her spirit animated her form.

I waited fifteen minutes, to give her time to check her things, get a drink and settle in, and then went looking for her. I found her sitting in a large, red leather armchair, her legs crossed, gloved hands on her knee, holding a riding crop. She seemed to be alone.

She had on tight-fitting black leather pants and a vest that looked like a corset, which admirably hoisted and displayed her ample breasts. Soon enough my eyes found their way down to her stylish, kid-leather ankle boots—size seven, I guessed. Her hair was dark and full, falling just below her shoulders, silky. With her petite face and soft tan skin, dark blue eyes and a voluptuous mouth, she was of ambiguous descent. Spanish was my closest guess. She looked to be in her late twenties or early thirties.

I went on one knee.

She looked at me curiously. Her dark, round eyes and moist, smiling lips confronted me, as if to say, *Show me something I haven't seen before.* She exuded complete confidence and had no fear of disappointing any man. Her heart was open.

"Would you like a foot massage?" I asked.

I could smell her freshness now and the thought of having her warm, moist feet in my hands gave me pleasure comparable to torture.

"The question is, do you want to massage them?" She replied.

She looked me up and down, cool as ice. She playfully sipped from the drink she held in her tightly-gloved hand, then merely moved her chin in what passed for a nod, and extended one of her crossed legs to offer me her boot.

Kneeling, I sat back on my heels. Slowly, I took her boot in my hands and kissed it firmly, smelling her and tasting the leather, sharp and salty. I could feel her toes through the leather, wriggling against my lips. I had untied hundreds of boots, massaged hundreds of feet, kissing and licking them until I knew I could never get enough. So far, this experience had surpassed any of the others, and I had yet to get her boots off. In spite of her beauty it was her unnameable, invisible, emanating spirit that drove me to the floor and nailed me there at her feet. I felt a connection that was more than just physical.

I pulled the boot off to reveal a small shapely foot in a thin white sock with a faint leather stain on the bottom, outlining her toes and arch. I reverently pressed my face to the top of her toes and breathed her in, drawing the life from her, pausing momentarily but not yet taking it upon myself to kiss her. She smelled sweetly of flowers and leather.

"May I please kiss?" I asked most respectfully.

She nodded, sipped from her drink, her eyes on me.

With a methodical, lustful passion I covered her warm foot with kisses, both top and bottom. I moved myself around her foot so as not to cause her discomfort or inconvenience, breathing her in and tasting her saltiness through her sock. She began to move and flex her foot, and I responded, caressing and kissing it more fervently.

"May I have your feet bare?" I asked. She smiled and nodded, gesturing toward her toes. I peeled off her sticky sock to reveal her smooth, moist, creamy skin, her strong heel and lovely, delicate arch. Her toes were full and straight. Even unpainted her toenails resembled candy. I couldn't contain my enthusiasm and dove in.

I massaged her with my hands, tongue and lips, starting at her heel and working forward, careful not to tickle, ending with her toes. I took each one into my mouth, sucking all of them hard to relieve them of the stress from the day and from being shod in those boots. I massaged each toe's bottom with my tongue, darting my tongue between them so as not to miss a single, precious morsel. I dreaded the moment it would all be over, and all the while gave heartfelt thanks for the gift bestowed upon me. But then I remembered there was another foot left, still in her ankle boot. I finished up and put her sock and boot back on and began with the other.

    I was overwhelmed by her presence: her scent was intoxicating. As I held her to my face, I asked what perfume she wore.

    "None," she answered, smiling lavishly, showing a row of straight, white teeth. "That's me you smell."

    I was working on getting the other boot unlaced when she caught the eye of a woman at the bar and called her over.

    "This is Sam, and I'm Lara, by the way," she said as Sam sat on the arm of Lara's red leather chair.

    "Mathew," I said, extending my hand to shake each of theirs.

    "He shakes my hand after twenty minutes licking my feet," Lara said to Sam. They laughed.

Sam was butch and had on chaps over jeans and a motorcycle jacket. She had short blond hair and slight features. She was attractive but tough-looking, like she partied and drank too much. She asked what Lara and I wanted and went back to the bar to get the three of us some more drinks.

"Are you a Cancer, Mathew? Lara asked.

"Yeah," I said, surprised that she had me pegged. "And you?"

Lara stirred her drink with the straw, which she held with two fingers, and looked me straight in the eyes.

"I'm a Pisces, Mathew. You should know that," she answered, and laughed a little to herself.

I knew little about astrology but I did know that each sign is assigned a body part and that Pisceans rule the feet.

Lust and zeal unabated, I worshipped Lara there. She got into it more and more and began exposing certain parts of her foot for me to attend to, sometimes pulling her foot away and denying me for a tantalizing moment.

I soon realized it would be polite, however, to finish up and leave Lara with Sam. I also had friends of my own to see. I put on her sock and boot, kissing both again, and struggled up. The idea of leaving my spot on the floor was distasteful to me because I knew it was where I belonged. Lara leaned forward and offered me her cheek to kiss, and I willingly complied. I also held and kissed her gloved hands, turning them over to kiss her palms.

"Where are you going to be?" Lara asked, a little flustered. She was not so cool, not nearly as collected as before. Her lips were pursed, her gaze went right through me. She sat upright in her chair, leaned forward and took hold of my leash. The same powerful magnetic essence that drew me to her earlier now stripped away my plans for the night and held me there by her.

"It was my intent to give you two time together," I told Lara shakily. "If it pleases you I should like to stay here—where I belong."

With that Lara smiled and sat back, relaxing now, eyes glistening. She stroked the leash and turned it over with one gloved hand, running the other through my hair.

It was that simple.

I REMEMBER A KINDERGARTEN CLASS, ALL OF US boys and girls sitting in a circle on the floor. My friend beside me reached for his foot, brought it up and bit his shoe. The next moment I was looking at a girl across the circle, Carla, who had her shoes off. I could see the bottom of her socks and on them the dirty outline of her feet. I wanted to hold them, to smell them. Her socks were powder blue.

For years I innocently dreamed of Carla's little feet. I would lie in bed and wish I were with her, under her covers, keeping her feet warm with kisses, with my cheeks. At school it drove me mad to see her pretty feet hidden by her shoes. I dreamed of her taking off her shoes so I could see her feet. I imagined them warm, moist and smelling infinitely sweet.

A fetish is defined as a sexual attraction to an inanimate object, but to me, a woman's feet have always been anything but inanimate. Who animates them and how they are animated has always been their greatest attraction for me. Fixation might be a better word. Whether it is a fixation for feet, sex, marriage or money, it doesn't matter. It all comes from the same place: the mind. There are countless reasons for developing fetishes, fixations and preferences, and often the differences are subtle. The one thing they share in common is that, at some point, the person has been exposed to an idea, and their mind has attached itself to associated thoughts and feelings and then has closed down around them, cementing itself to these ideas.

Slowly, I noticed other girls and their feet, too: schoolmates, company that came over to the house, strangers. Repression inevitably creates further expansion of the fixation, and there isn't much a little boy can do to understand and satisfy his love for pretty feet.

Lara had my number. For the first five days after meeting her at the fet night I sat by the phone whenever I could. It was unlike anything I had experienced with a woman before. Lara had made such a strong impression on me that night that I found myself feeling desperate not to lose her.

    I was in the bath when she finally called. I ran out to get the phone, dripping, and brought it back with me. We talked until the water got cold. It was a normal conversation considering how we had met. We discussed everyday things that are not brought up in the midst of fantasy.

    Lara was younger than I had thought—twenty-three. She had moved to Toronto from Vancouver five years earlier and was finishing up a degree in Commerce. She was living with Sam and they were romantically involved, but

Lara intimated theirs was an open relationship. I sensed tension in that supposed openness. I don't know what made me think she would have anything to do with me, a man. I only knew that I wanted to be with her.

Lara found out I was twenty-five and worked on Bay Street in low-level administration, and that my pursuits were oriented not toward career but rather toward the personal and the spiritual. I found the conversation strained when we dipped too far into the past or got too personal. While I mentioned that I was from Saskatoon, from a large family with amazing parents who had become my friends over the years, she had little to say about her home, except that one of her brothers was in jail. Nonetheless, we had a great time during our conversation, and I was thrilled to learn whatever I could about this wonderful woman.

As far back as I could remember, I'd had dreams of having a beautiful, spirited, sexy dominant woman like Lara in my life, but wondered if it was at all possible. Fantasy, without anything concrete, is a rigid script that is difficult to cast. A submissive man will fantasize all his life about what he wants, and eventually he needs those exact fantasies played out. I saw this in my friends in the fetish scene and wondered how it applied to me. These desires become the bars of our cage.

There was part of me that had dreaded the phone conversation with Lara. I was afraid that whatever affinity we had experienced at fet night was fleeting. Luckily, I discovered my fears were for nothing and I hung up feeling hopeful and in love. I knew that I was soulfully bound to Lara.

For weeks after our conversation, I could think of nothing else. I masturbated regularly to thoughts of Lara: her lips and mouth, her eyes, hair and fragrance, her hands and feet. She was more than a fantasy to me. I noticed no other women, except to see them pale in comparison.

We began spending time together, casually at first, although I was dying for more. One afternoon I met Lara downtown for lunch. It was a warm, humid day. Lara wore a light, blue, summer dress and had on matching four-and-a-half-inch heels, no stockings, no make-up. She also wore a delicate silver necklace and matching earrings. She was breathtaking. After lunch she wanted to see where I lived so I took her by streetcar to the West End, to my place in High

Park. My apartment was a clean, inexpensive third-floor bachelor. It had a few small windows, but I had it well lit and warmly decorated so it was quite a cozy little space. Lara inspected it thoroughly with her sharp, feminine eye. I felt she was assessing me, not the apartment.

Satisfied with whatever she had learned, she sat on my sofa while I went to the fridge for something to drink. When I brought her lemonade, she kicked off her heels and put her feet up beside her. I knelt there next to her, at her feet.

Lara brought one of her feet to my mouth and I kissed it. She was hot and tasted salty. Lara reached for the magazine rack next to the sofa, took up a magazine I collected and began flipping through it while I indulged myself at her feet—the first time since we had met at fet night. I nibbled at her sweaty soles. Not a single callous. So tender. No matter how I tried I could not lick and suck from them the smell of leather. I looked up and Lara's eyes met mine. It was pure experience. I was enraptured.

I rubbed peppermint cream onto Lara's feet to cool them. She watched me pay homage to her but said nothing. I innocently went above the ankle with the cream but she stopped me, scolding, "No, no, no," while playfully waving a finger at me.

Her mission completed, Lara gathered herself to leave, telling me that she and Sam were going out for dinner. She didn't seem too happy about it. I began to wonder what exactly was her mission. I sensed that she enjoyed spending time with me, and was even getting turned on by my worship, but that something in her was fighting it.

"I'm going to teach you to give a proper manicure and pedicure, Mathew," Lara said as she hugged me and kissed my cheek on her way out the door.

But when?

Lara and I saw each other a few more times after she let me have her feet for the second time. My relationship with her was becoming one of unrequited love and obsession. I was growing desperate while she remained aloof, toying with me. She would tell me to call her at a certain time, then wouldn't be home. She would have me meet her someplace and then wouldn't show up herself. When we finally would get together, it was as if she were not there, as though she had someplace, anyplace else to be. And worst of all, she had been denying me her feet ever since that afternoon in my apartment.

I was reaching my boiling point. I called Lara one morning at our predetermined time. Once more she wasn't home, or wasn't answering. As the answering machine clicked on, I pictured her in bed making ravenous love to anyone but me. I was at the end of my tether.

"Look, Lara, this is one time too many that you've cancelled plans or aren't home. I've had it. Obviously you don't care about me. I can't go on like this. If you ever wish to take me seriously give me a call." I hung up the phone.

I felt awful, heartbroken. I'd only ever been kind and gentle with her, but it didn't seem to matter. While I had always longed to be taken and used, I wanted it to be with inclusion and affection. Instead, she was shutting me out.

At first I felt good about my decision; deep down, I knew I was right. Yet, facing the prospect of life without Lara, I felt dismembered, incomplete. I was too proud to go crawling to her if her aloofness was intended out of spite, and not as part of the subservient relationship I longed for. I silently hoped she would call, or that I would see her at another fet night. Whenever I saw a message light on my answering machine, I prayed it was from Lara. I felt her drawing me in, and although I picked up the phone a few times, I just couldn't bring myself to call her. I wanted to be her slave, not her fool.

When I was twelve, I fell for a girl one year behind me at school named Susan. I had a huge crush on her, and for the first time, thoughts of sex entered my mind, meshing together, of course, with my fully developed love for feet. One day, in the coat room, I found myself staring dumbly at her as she sat on the bench pulling off her boots, her soiled white socks so thin I could see her smooth, sweaty skin and her blue toenail polish through them. *Candies, treats,* I thought as I caught a glimpse of her little toes. I looked up to find that she had caught me staring at her, and I couldn't look away. She had high, Slavic cheekbones, straight teeth, full, moist lips, a flawless complexion and beautiful eyes. I wanted to be with her so badly even though I wasn't quite sure what I would have done with her.

  I thought about Susan all the time. In my

fantasies she would sit firm and tall while I knelt to kiss her feet. I began to envision her making me earn my pleasure by having me "perform" for her: carrying her books, cleaning her room and polishing her muddy boots. It is not always true that a foot fetish will lead to fantasies of submissiveness, but it is common and it happened to me. Wanting to be down at her feet, attending to the lowest, dirtiest part of her, led me that way. My mind closed further around the fantasy.

I had my first girlfriend at fourteen. My family spent summers at Waskesiu, in Prince Albert National Park. We had a small, portable cabin lined up among the others. Each was painted a different colour, row upon row. It was a great place to spend summers because in the nearby town there was a theatre, roller-skating rink, an ice-cream parlour and a gorgeous beach with lots of kids my age hanging around.

Consistent with my past crushes, my attraction to Jennifer began physically, with her feet. The first time I saw her she caught my eye. She was slim with long, dirty-blonde hair and always wore a pair of filthy runners with holes in them, through which I could see her equally filthy socks. My attraction to her was overpowering.

That summer Jennifer and I dated like teenagers do. We hiked, roller-skated, swam, went to movies, and snuggled a lot. Even though this was enough for me, I still fixated on her feet and longed to hold them.

I remember going to the beach and seeing her bare feet for the first time. I couldn't sit still. *What would she do if I just kissed them?* I wondered. She sat beside me on her towel, digging little trenches in the wet sand with her heels, her tiny toes pointed upwards. I would have given anything to take each toe into my mouth and suck it clean, sand and all.

One night while we were at a movie, Jennifer was sitting with one ankle resting across her knee, her foot close to me, moving up and down to the beat of the score. It seemed that my heart was beating a thousand times a minute. I reached over and put my hand on her shoe, then ran it up to her ankle. I felt her warm sock. My heart wanted to explode, either from the fear or from the excitement I felt at being so close to my fantasy.

At the end of the summer we each went home to our separate cities and wrote to keep in touch. In one of my letters I told her how I wanted to hold her, and how I wanted to caress and kiss her feet.

    I never heard from her again.

As I progressed through adolescence, I became shy. I had a hard time communicating to girls what it was that I wanted. Around this time some of my friends were beginning to have girlfriends and sex, but I never felt like I was missing out on anything they were getting. What I needed was completely different, I thought, and I doubted they could get it either, had they been in my place. As time went on I saw myself getting desperate, so I averted my attention away from dating. I withdrew. I simply spent my time at school with friends and tried not to think about realizing my desires.

    Literature became my outlet. I read *The Story of O,* as well as some other erotica titles like *Venus In Furs*, by Leopold Von Sacher-Masoch, from whom the term masochist is derived. In real life, Sacher-Masoch was a nobleman who gave up his position to be a slave to the mistress of his dreams, his Venus in Furs. This was before 1850! As he begged his mistress to enslave him she would tell him to be careful, that he might get what he's asking for. I also perused seedier stuff and began to read about domineering women and how they put their slaves into bondage, how they disciplined them and trained them to serve and worship. These women kept real slaves! These fantasies built upon what I already felt. They were powerful, intoxicating. I began to wonder how I might meet the Mistress of my dreams, or if this was even possible.

Fet nights had found permanent homes at Boots nightclub just off Yonge Street and a couple of spots on Sherbourne Street. I continued to go to them because I needed my release. Truthfully, I always hoped that I might run into Lara again.

    I met Alex at fet night. She was trim and hard, with incredible muscular definition. She had shoulder length, dirty-blonde hair, fair skin and bright green eyes. She was just a partygoer, like me, and not a professional dominatrix. We played that first night: I was allowed her feet if she could put me on the bench and whip me. She wore a pink PVC halter, chaps and pink leather cowgirl boots, size five. She whipped me first, starting off gentle and sensuous, then building the pace slowly. She was an expert.

    "I'm working up a nice sweat," she said to me through her breath. She brought her foot to rest on the bench where I could see it. "Kiss my boot," she commanded.

I did.

"There's a delectable treat waiting for you in there," Alex taunted, "if you behave. Will you behave?"

"Yes," I answered, hoping I'd know what "behave" meant when the time came.

Alex upped the tempo and chastised me whenever I made a demonstration of my pain. I learned to immerse myself in it and the myriad sensations that came with it. The whipping became its own reward, to the point where I felt I didn't need Alex's feet. I got them anyhow and they were glorious. I spent an hour lapping at every tasty morsel of sweat she'd worked up while whipping me.

I knew from the start of our relationship that I'd never mean much to Alex. Her actions were calculated to keep me at arm's-length, no matter what we ended up doing together. Our dates were all about sex, always at her place in Cabbagetown in the East End, and allotted exclusively at her discretion. If we had dinner, it was always at her place, before or after sex. All of this was fine with me at the time. It seemed to me that she lived her life in the fast lane, and this was something that I didn't want to become too involved in. Still, she had it all and could become her partner's every fantasy, especially since it was for her own gratification.

    The first time we fucked Alex absolutely ravaged me. I had gone to get her some groceries for dinner, and when I got back, she had on nothing except for a pair of red, five-inch heels. She stripped me down and took me to the washroom, where she lathered and shaved me from upper lip to small toe, then dragged the new, smooth me into her living room. She threw me down and ground the sole of her stiletto into my face and made me lick the sharp heels clean. Then she kicked the shoes off and ran one foot and then the other over my face, my chest, my cock and balls, while I writhed in joyful agony, secretly begging for release. She pulled me up and brought my face to her vulva and proceeded to teach me the finer points of oral sex. I did as she instructed. Alex came three or four times while I tongued her. I was rock hard. She saw this and rolled a condom down me and mounted me. She rode me expertly and defied me to come until she said I could. Squeezing every bit of usefulness from me, Alex enjoyed yet another deep, vaginal orgasm.

    She sat motionless with me still inside

her and ready to burst. I could feel her squeezing me, her muscles rippling up and down. She made me beg for it, truly beg. Beg I did, like a kid for candy. Finally, she allowed me to climax and my orgasm washed over me for what seemed forever. That's what Alex did—she brought out the best in you.

Afterwards, Alex got up to get us some wine and I moved to the sofa, waiting for her return. There, on the back cushion, was a dry semen stain. *Did Alex ever rest?* I wondered, realizing it couldn't be mine.

While sex with Alex met all of my physical desires, there was still something important missing. I had just celebrated my twenty-sixth birthday and found myself pulling away from fet parties a bit to try to date women who were outside of the scene. Through a few of these non-fet relationships, I discovered that while I was confident and aggressive in the world of fetish, I was shaky and self-conscious with "normal" women. They seemed to be looking for stability, and I was afraid they wouldn't understand or be able to fulfill my sexual needs.

I often thought of Lara then. In my soul there was unfinished business, an emptiness that could not be sorted out long-distance. I found myself again on my own, going down the same old road. Despite a few brief relationships that I'd had outside the scene, I was back at fetish nights within a few months. I tried to get into it again, but underlying the scene was a shallow sameness. Different people, same thing. I needed someone with whom I could dig deep, with whom I could find the wellspring. I was dying of thirst.

My first love had appeared in my early twenties. I was still living in Saskatoon, and I had just opened a relaxation spa. I had a regular customer, whom I got to know over time, named Debra. She was a natural blonde, with bright blue eyes and a beautiful smile. She was several years older than I. The first time she entered my spa she removed her high heels and pranced barefoot up to the reception desk. Her toenails were painted red and her feet were well cared for. She was outgoing and friendly. I was instantly smitten.

  We got to know each other through the business and my feelings for her grew stronger every time I saw her. My rocky dating experiences up to this point had made me wary, though, and I didn't want to jeopardize the friendship with Debra by telling her how I felt about her. Also, she was a customer and I felt I should be professional about it. But as I got to know her, my feelings overwhelmed me. I was blinded by my desire for her and I longed for my desires to be fulfilled, not to remain hidden and unexpressed. There were many sleepless nights I would lie awake thinking of her, wishing to have her, fearing she'd pass me by. So I wrote her a letter. I told her how I felt, how I wanted to make love to her. Somewhere in that letter I told her how beautiful her feet were—after all, she was a Pisces. I was thrilled she didn't run when she got my letter. Instead, she came to me.

We started seeing each other regularly. We went to her favourite bar every weekend, rented movies, cooked and had dinner together. She was cautious and took things at her own pace, but I knew she had feelings for me.

The first time we slept together was the first time I had ever had release. She had already kicked off her heels, and her soles were soiled and stained almost permanently from dancing and sweating all night. As she lay on my bed I knelt there, rapturous, hardly able to breath. Here was my first pair of feet.

Could my first be more lovely? I wondered to myself.

It was everything I had expected. Debra

was beautiful, and to look up into her dreamy face, to see her lovely eyes and to hear her moans, her pleasure, was more than I could bear. I had never given a proper foot massage before, so I just bathed her feet with my tongue and lips, stopping only to kiss her beautiful face. She smelled slightly of sweat and leather, and no matter how long and diligently I lapped and sucked and nibbled at her feet, I couldn't clean the stains from their bottoms. I couldn't get enough. My attentions were driving her around the bend so she asked me to move upward. I complied, but I must admit that, at that time, her feet were where my skills, but not my passions, began and ended.

Our relationship blossomed. We became close friends, happy to just hang around together. When we did go out, I had as much fun watching her put on her make-up and getting dressed as I did going out with her. Being around her dressing table, high heels, stockings and clothes was novel to me. I had never been that close to a woman before.

Debra fuelled all my submissive fantasies. I dreamed of her dressing room and wardrobe and longed to have them to care for. I asked her a couple of times if I could tidy her home for her, but she declined. She felt uncomfortable with that. I also asked if I could take care of her feet for her. She had me give her a pedicure and foot bath only once. I remember her showing me some basics and then just relaxing with a glass of white wine while I worked away. But all this was a boon. Just to be able to ask meant the world to me. Finally a woman who didn't think I was nuts. She actually liked to hear me talk about my fantasies, even if she was reluctant to act all of them out for me.

    I had secured my family's cabin at Waskesiu for a couple of days and asked her along. She was eyeing me throughout the two-and-a-half-hour drive. I got one bag in through the door and she was all over me, tearing my clothes off, throwing me down on the bed and riding me. She thrusted my face between her legs and writhed there for a while until she needed me inside her again. We made love like that for hours. She never stopped coming at me, and I surrendered willingly. Toward the end we were getting numb. We had to make a conscious effort to stop ourselves. It was my first pure experience as a result of sex.

    I discovered that Debra had her own fantasies. She was somewhat submissive herself and asked me a few times to spank her and to tie her to the bed. I wanted to do these things for her but they just didn't excite me. I became so uninterested in it that I couldn't even find the energy to go through the motions, even for her sake. I was too obsessed with my own needs.

After slightly more than a year together, our relationship was becoming strained. Our age difference and the incompatibility of our similar fantasies of submission soon began to affect Debra. She began to pull herself away from me and finally explained it to me as best she could. She said she loved me, that I was her soul mate, but that there were other considerations that were important to her at this stage in her life. She realized that I still had to experience things that she was finished with. We agreed to remain friends, and although I took it hard at first, I soon began to come to terms with it.

After some grief and introspection, the pattern of my responsiveness became clear to me, though it would be some years before I fully grasped it. I needed an aggressive woman to take control of me. When I thought about the situations where Debra was aggressive, like she was that time at the cabin, I couldn't imagine my sex drive being stronger or sex being better. But when Debra was the one who needed to be acted upon, who needed to be thrown down and taken, my heart wasn't in it. I felt nothing at all. I finally knew what I needed, but where could I begin to find it?

One bleak Saturday afternoon the phone rang.

"Hello?"

"Hi."

It was a woman's voice, someone I'd met at a fetish party, I assumed.

"Mathew?"

"Yeah. Who's this?"

There was a momentary pause.

"Lara."

It took a few seconds for this to register in my mind. I'd resigned myself to wanting Lara but thought she'd never call. I actually allowed it be part of my fantasy of her using me as she wished: she could have me when she wanted or lock me away when she didn't. I needed for her to call and I guess she figured that out.

My throat swelled and I had a hard time speaking. I had to sit down. I knew how proud she was, how hard it must have been for her to pick up the phone. In my eyes, the call alone did her apologizing. It didn't occur to me at the time that it was possible that she was calling for her own sake, not mine; that she wanted to make peace because she couldn't stand someone not liking her.

It had been almost a year since I had left the message on her answering machine, but we spoke for hours, as if we'd never been apart.

"Do you have a Mistress yet?"

There was a vulnerability to her when she asked this that was alien to such a seemingly confident and remarkable woman.

"*You* are my Mistress," I told her. "Always have been, always will be. You know that."

Lara and I began seeing each other regularly after that phone call. We were becoming friends and it was all very normal. We grew familiar, did all the regular things, such as going to movies, having dinner together, shopping (I bought her shoes for her now), and going to the bar where she worked. Except it felt a bit on the sly. Even though we weren't sexually involved, she didn't want her girlfriends talking. I learned that I was the only man in her life, and only the second ever. She was a lady's lady. But nothing is ever so cut and dry. Sam, for example, the ultimate butch, had had several male lovers.

Lara and I started to bond physically. She began to utilize me, instructing me to care for her hands and feet, and even allowing me to come over and do half of her chores while Sam was out. She brought me to a few fet nights and had fun leashing me around but would never let me have her feet there, or anywhere. "Stop asking for my feet, Mathew. I know you want them," she would say when I hounded her for them. This annoyed me somewhat. I couldn't figure out whether she was uninterested or somehow denying her true desires. If it was her tactic of handling me, it wasn't working very well.

There were a lot of people in her life. I was just one. She wanted to manage me properly this time, and calculated her every move. One sunny Saturday afternoon a few months after we had begun seeing each other again, I took Lara to a sell-off at a theatrical supply house where she bought several costumes for herself. She was thrilled. After that, we went for brunch at an outdoor patio on Church Street, in the gay neighbourhood. The trees were blooming and the air was uncommonly fresh for downtown. Midway through the meal she sprung her question on me.

"Let's get a place together," she suggested.

I was astounded. I knew that she had been thinking of putting distance between herself and Sam, and of course I'd dreamed of us being together, but her life and her women made it appear just that, a dream.

"Are you serious?" I asked.

She was frustrated that I hadn't thrown myself at her feet then and there.

"Yes, I'm serious," she said self-consciously.

I knew there were two or three women begging Lara to move in with them. Why not them, if she just wanted to take some time off from Sam? I couldn't understand her motive.

"Why me?" I asked. "What about Sam? Look, you've surprised me with this, that's all."

"You don't want to move in with me," Lara stated, disappointed.

I'd never seen her look hurt before. I took her hand.

"There's a lot to consider." I joked, "You have a cat. I'm allergic to cats."

"Fine," she said flatly.

"Why me? Why not one of your girlfriends?"

"Look," she began, "each one of them had a chance to have me and they blew it by screwing around and lying. Now I do what I want. I refuse to be pinned down by any of them. And platonic is not possible. They always end up wanting me and hating everyone else in my life because of it. Even Sam has been driving me crazy. Listen, Mathew," Lara said, squeezing my hand hard, "we get along, we love each other."

"The problem is, you don't love me nearly as much as I love you, not in the same way," I pointed out. I couldn't believe how bullheaded I was being. "I'm not sure I could handle seeing lover after lover passing by me either," I managed to say.

Lara sighed.

"If we had some kind of arrangement, something that was ours alone, I might get by," I offered.

The waitress came with the check and Lara took her purse and went through it, looking for her wallet.

"Just what kind of arrangement?" she asked while fumbling through her things. She found her wallet and put some money on the table.

"I have to be able to express my love for you my way, which means—"

"You're serious about this Mistress thing, aren't you?"

"Why not? It's perfectly suited to you. Think about it for a minute." I found it hard to believe she hadn't taken me seriously. "Fetish and s/m have always been a sidebar for you, with women. You obviously seem to want some kind of a relationship with a man. And this is perfect for us. You could be my Mistress, I could be your slave."

The words came out dry. It had always been my hope to be taken and now it was like I was taking myself. But I didn't care. This was my dream, I couldn't let it pass me by.

"I think we can arrange that," Lara said mischievously.

It occurred to me then that perhaps it was her fantasy to have me ask for it.

SHORTLY AFTER BREAKING UP WITH DEBRA, I HAD to close my spa because of some poor business planning. The business had been breaking even but I didn't have enough money to buy essentials like groceries. I simply hadn't had enough in reserve to start with.

    The break with Debra, the loss of my job and a deep dissatisfaction with my inability to either escape or fulfill my desires left me aimless. I found myself asking a lot of questions—who I was, what I wanted, where I was going—an introspective headspace I've always turned to in tough times.

    My questioning began early and naturally, when I was eleven or twelve. I was raised as a Roman Catholic. I remember a priest telling me "God has always been and will always be." I would often lie in bed wondering how anything could exist forever, or what it meant "to be." I thought that God must originate from nothing but, as the age-old question goes, how could something come from nothing? I tried wrapping my mind around that. As a result, I grew up questioning the world, its religion and politics, the way we perceive war, violence, world hunger, marriage, work, sex—things that seemed obvious to a lot of people. I read a lot, followed current events and studied history. I saw great inconsistencies in what was happening and what people said and believed. I found that life for me was hollow if I didn't face all kinds of issues, even the most negative events and thoughts. I wanted to live fully, not hiding in a shell, afraid to come out.

Part of what prodded me along in my natural inclination to question was a hereditary bone disease that I was born with, multiple exostoses. The condition is characterized by benign tumours on the skeleton, excluding the skull and spine. The growths have a tendency to get in the way of normal tissue and limb movement, and thus need to be removed. The first tumours were removed when I was nine, from my ribcage and hip. (I would have six operations and thirteen incisions in the future, and two dozen or more tumours taken out.) Most came off my legs. Many more remain.

My doctors have said throughout the years that there is a five-percent chance any growth could turn cancerous. This risk got me thinking and questioning early. I knew that I had only the present moment, that there was no time to waste. I came to understand over the years that, in reality all any of us have is this moment, this "now." That this moment is both eternal and infinite: all is contained within it, always in constant flux. My condition drove this home. It made me want to do what I needed to do. I knew I might never get to be an old man tapping his cane saying, "I wish…"

Despite my constant questioning, I had never considered or encountered meditation until I was in my early twenties. I happened upon an article in *Sports Fitness* on flotation tanks, which are soundproof, lightproof, gravity-altered environments used for relaxation, self-hypnosis and injury recovery. The article said that floating in a solution of Epsom salts and water, which is one hundred times more buoyant than the Dead Sea, causes blood to flow more freely, stress to be taken off joints and muscles, and thoughts to become difficult to hang on to. These are the same effects achieved while a person's mind is properly engaged in meditation. I loved the idea, and within six months I opened my relaxation spa that offered this technology, below a doctor's office.

    I floated regularly, sometimes for up to three hours at a time. It was physically relaxing, and sure enough, was a sort of forced meditation, allowing me to simply *be* in the quiet spaciousness. Sensory input is at a minimum when you are floating. I could barely feel the silky, skin-temperature solution on my body. All I could hear was the blood coursing through my vessels with each heartbeat, and my eyeballs grinding away in their sockets as they rolled beneath closed lids. While floating in what seemed like almost nothingness, I lost connection with my former perception of my body, who I thought I was. *What am I then?* I asked myself. *What is this?*

    These were really the same questions in different form that I'd asked at age twelve. Somehow they stuck with me. All my questions fell into one, *What is this?* I knew instinctively that answering that one question would answer all the others. These questions and the practice of focusing my mind on them became important sources of stability among all the other changes that had been happening in my life.

    Eventually I stumbled upon a book called *The Three Pillars of Zen* by Phillip

Kapleau, which is an A-B-C guide to the practice of Zen meditation. Flipping through it, I found references to koans, which are spiritual questions that come naturally or are assigned by a Zen master. I realized then that my natural questions—*What am I? What is this?*—were my koans and that mediation could lead me to some answers. My affinity for Zen was immediate. I bought the book and immediately attempted the *zazen,* or Zen meditation. But I found it quite hard to sustain a focused mind for any length of time. I decided to write to the author. His assistant reached me from Rochester, New York, and informed me of a Zen centre in Toronto led by one of Kapleau's former students. The pull was strong. I felt a group setting was what I needed to take my questioning further. Underneath this motive, however, was the secret hope that the large city and the subcultures that I figured must exist there would allow me room to breathe.

  Without Debra and without employment I studied my options: I packed my Datsun 210 and was off to Toronto.

My stuff was packed and moved in two hours. Lara's belongings took a week for her to pack, and then a month for *me* to unpack. She had four chests of drawers, a walk-in closet and two regular closets full of her clothes. She asked me to see if I'd missed anything and I found twelve more garment bags in the garage! I helped her organize her wardrobe, bought and assembled a canopy bed for her and painted her room forest green as she requested.

  Our home was a small, two-bedroom, two-storey house on Palmerston Boulevard, right off of College Street. It was a great location: plenty of restaurants and bars, good shopping and a second-run movie theatre nearby. It was close to my job on Bay Street, and affordable for both of us, even with Lara still in school and working at the bar. Our apartment had never been renovated as had many in the neighbourhood, but it had been well maintained. There were natural-wood doors and window frames, and a fireplace in the living room. There was a small lawn in the front and a garage in back. It was my first real home, and it was ours.

Lara did most of the initial cleaning. She was an expert and had me there to learn her tricks.

"I'll tell you once, show you once," she said to me. "Then it's up to you."

Lara's lovers began to arrive within that first week and she timed them perfectly: when one went out the back door to her car, another came in the front from the streetcar. Never a slip-up. I heard Lara telling them to never show up early or late, they were to come and leave when told. No arguments. Period. Her approach to her lovers shocked me and took me by surprise. It seemed rather cold and unfeeling. I wondered what I had gotten myself into and brought it up with Lara. I tried to be tactful.

"It's none of your business, Mathew," she said, angered but not raising her voice. "I told you, they had their chance. Now, it's my way or the highway. If they don't like it, they can leave."

"Do they know about each other?"

"Mathew!" she said, her voice rising an octave or two. "It's none of your business."

"I think it is. We're starting a relationship of our own. I'm in a vulnerable spot. I have to know I can trust you. Are you being honest with these women? Are you letting them know what it is they can take or leave?"

I was right to question Lara on this matter, but in my desire to make it work and my need to be with her, I allowed her arguments to sink in and I sided with her. Still, I told myself I'd never let happen to me what was happening to her girlfriends.

I was ignored those first three months. Lara could sense that it bothered me from my distance and my sulking, and denied me her feet for a week as a punishment. It turned out to be the longest week of my life. The whole while Lara received lover after lover after lover. But that didn't bother me in the least because by denying me, Lara was at least handling me, and that was a step in the right direction in her role as my Mistress. From the time that Lara asked me to move in with her I knew that the key to my accepting her lifestyle and lovers was the degree to which she would treat me as her slave, and how much time she would spend with me as my Mistress. In denying me her feet, Lara was acting as my Mistress.

It wasn't that I cared about what she did

or who she did it with, it was that her occasional denial or punishment wasn't enough. I could have easily accepted her lovers if she would have handled me. I was impatient, I wanted to move the pace of our relationship up a notch, to see Lara spend more time cultivating our Mistress/slave relationship. But I was powerless to move at any pace other than Lara's. She didn't appreciate my comments on the matter, and therefore, I had no outlet. I would watch her endless parade of lovers, day after day, and stew. For me there was next to nothing.

I told her my feelings, how I thought our Mistress/slave relationship should progress, and that it would be unbearable for me otherwise. All that came of my honesty was the understanding that Lara didn't like to be told what to do. It robbed her of her energy to want to do anything. This was my Catch-22. If it wasn't her idea, she might dismiss it forever. Shortly after this conversation, though, Lara did formally instruct me on the performance of her domestic chores, which until then had been haphazard.

Foremost was Lara's wardrobe. She taught me what to press and how. She wanted me to attend to the constant polish and repair of her footwear. Her room also had to be just so: her bed was to be made when I got home from work; her sex toys had to be cleaned and put away. She left no detail unrehearsed. She saw everything.

All general housework and yardwork became my domain, except when the work wasn't up to her standards. I cooked for her three or four nights a week, and most mornings I served her breakfast in bed before I went to work. No matter who had shown up the night before, Lara always woke alone.

There was no end to the work Lara had for me. Aside from regular daily, weekly and monthly duties, there was always something that needed painting, hanging or readjusting. Lara had good taste and impeccable awareness. She knew if I had missed a spot with the vacuum. I know this because I tested her. She seemed to tolerate some poor effort on my part. My reward was the work itself, and her feet, but for those I had to beg.

A privilege for me was being able to attend to Lara's body—a true reward. Lara bought me all the tools to take care of her hands and feet, including a beautiful pink etched-glass bowl for soaking her feet. She also bought me an expensive antique carrying case to hold all the manicure and pedicure equipment, which I kept with me in my room. She made me her masseur and purchased a glossy hardcover book on the art and made me study it. Lara taught me how to care for her, her way. She adored sculpting me, molding me to anticipate her quirks and whims. I loved her for this and my excitement for her made me infinitely pliable. I was under her heel, where I felt I truly belonged.

"It could take a lifetime," she said to me once, regarding this training, "and may actually never end."

I began attending to her baths, pouring them, washing her back, shaving her legs, drying her body with one of her gargantuan terry cloth towels. Once while she stood in her bath as I patted her dry, she peed. It was vintage Lara: a natural, erotic act, unbridled sexuality. It froze me. Mesmerized, I watched the gold liquid stream down to the bath water. Lara found the last drop with her fingertip and placed it on my tongue, which I had automatically offered up.

That tantalizing drop was the world to me. Fetish and s/m are not always about extremes; they are about creating and prolonging lust and desire. I begged incessantly to have her. "You never know what you can get if you behave," she would say.

These tasks—manicures, pedicures, massages—were our physical relationship then; they promised nothing more, and yet, they were whole and complete in and of themselves. I was content, but naturally, I did want more. Lara probably wanted it that way because it kept me striving. I hoped that some day Lara would have the heart to have me serve her orally. I wanted nothing more than to demonstrate for her what I could do. I had seen her down there, as she made no effort to hide herself around the house, and once she had even put me on my knees so I could look at her newly-pierced clitoris. Furthermore, aside from the pedicures, I didn't get to have Lara's feet nearly enough, only when I sincerely begged. When I finally was allowed them, it was a gift beyond all gifts. I was very grateful and therefore afraid to complain for fear that twice a week might become once a month, or worse, never. I didn't like to have to beg for Lara's feet. I wanted to be acted upon, taken, but Lara thought that it didn't make sense to force someone to do what he wants anyway.

At this time Lara was not actively controlling my orgasm. Alternately prohibiting and permitting the slave's sexual release is a key element to a Mistress owning and directing her slave's energy; it's included in all s/m manuals. She knew I wasn't interested in sex with anyone else and that I wouldn't have had the time, considering I was constantly performing one chore or another for her. She'd given me pictures of her, as well as worn stockings, shoes and panties from time to time, for me to masturbate to. But I had no control over myself. I was an animal, masturbating over her five to six times a day. I felt it was sapping me of energy, and that didn't serve her in any way. "Control my orgasm, control your slave," I told her.

She wasn't upset when I brought it up. She realized her experience with men was limited. What happened next was a pleasant surprise. Originally she forbade me to masturbate, preferring that as my punishment. She saw it as an opportunity to relinquish my will to her. She would simply ask daily if I had, and would know if I was lying. If I masturbated without her consent, I would be punished. Lara would never use an unimaginative punishment like bondage and whipping. She would consider that a reward to work toward. Punishment meant denial of her many and varied gifts, such as allowing me to massage her feet with my mouth or being allowed to rub cream into her hands. But she underestimated my penis' hold over me—she hadn't enough punishments in her book for all my misdeeds.

"Every time I deny you something," she said to me honestly, "I deny myself."

So she had me measured for a locking belt that would keep me from myself. It was made of leather, stainless steel and chain mail. It fit like a g-string, with the concealment device hanging loose and unnoticed under clothing. It allowed for erections but no relief of any kind. Lara was thrilled with it and with the ultimate denial it afforded.

"I fuck who I want, when I want, how I want, whenever I want," Lara said cheerily while I knelt by her bed. "You, on the other hand, can't even hope to jerk off unless I say so, and even then it will have to be in a manner dictated by me." With that, she laughed her crystalline laugh and rubbed her foot under my balls, just to ensure my total bliss.

I was happy and Lara seemed happy, too. She had freedom she'd never had, and her thorough use of me occupied my mind and gave me purpose. I saw clearly for the first time that I was the only constant in her life. Sam told me as much. It was not insignificant that a woman like Lara had let me into the most intimate parts of her life. I thought of that any time a twinge of jealousy came over me.

I HAD BEEN LIVING IN THE TORONTO ZEN CENTRE for nearly two years, and it was now 1990. I was frantic, sitting *zazen* all the time, attending every formal retreat I could. It was a beautiful temple, sparse but well kept and hinting towards a Japanese influence. There were a number of young people like me there, several of whom also lived as residents. There were formal sittings most mornings and evenings, and retreats every two to three months, each ranging in length from two to seven days.

Formal sitting takes place in a hall, or *zendo*, made for that purpose. A low platform, or *tan*, edges the room and there are mats and cushions on it. Practitioners sit in either the lotus or *seiza* positions, facing the wall, quietly focusing on their particular form of *zazen*. Moving about is not permitted as it distracts the mind and the other practitioners, but periodically, the *zendo* master will stride around the *tan*, "energizing" willing participants with a long stick. The periods of sitting last thirty-five minutes, with two to three rounds each night. A retreat, or *sesshin,* contains about ten hours of formal sitting each day. At these retreats practitioners are able to meet with the teacher, or *sensei,* to ask questions about their practice. These questions can be about physical problems while sitting in one of the formal positions, or they may be about the *zazen* itself and the mental states one may find oneself in while engaged in meditation. Usually there are three of these meetings, or *dokusan,* a day. For more advanced practitioners close to insight or enlightenment, these meetings are often a direct opportunity for the *sensei* to test the participant, to see if he or she has made progress.

    I was involved in formal koan practice. At this centre, practitioners who worked on koans were assigned an initial koan, one that they worked on for as long as it took them to answer. While one could answer the koans verbally, the practice insists that it is essential to live the answer, to demonstrate one's understanding. The answer is not of the rational mind: it is an organic experience, one which comes from the practitioner seeing into the emptiness of form, the form of emptiness. Once one has had this experience, subsequent koans are assigned. These are different from the initial koan: the answers to these are meant to expand and deepen the original experience. Without continued practice, the original experience recedes in memory and becomes difficult to live out.

My time at the centre was fruitful. The group sitting was quite powerful, but the pull of the fetish scene was strong, distracting. Living in Toronto exposed me to possibilities not available in Saskatoon. Gratification seemed close at hand and possible. I had read an ad for a fetish party thrown by Northbound Leather. I was terribly excited by this news. For weeks I envisioned what these parties would be like, what I might wear, what kind of women would attend. I was already hoping I might find a woman who would take and enslave me, who would do to me the kinds of things Debra had done, only all the time and with more intensity. I had to see if there was a woman like that out there.

I was beginning to realize that I was lonely in my life as Lara's servant. She hadn't named me her slave yet. As I surrendered to Lara, I saw everything and everyone else dropping away. Lara knew I had friends and told me I could see and talk to them, but there was so much to do for her that I couldn't spare ten minutes from my day without the possibility of displeasing her. Consequently, fear gripped me: I felt like I was in deep and there wasn't much I could do about it. This was my life. I'd made a commitment and had to stick with it. I needed to discuss it with Lara rather than brood about it, but I was even more afraid of that. She hated it when things didn't go smoothly on their own.

Lara worked a few nights a week bartending and DJ-ing, all while finishing her Bachelor of Commerce degree. She made decent tips, at least as much as I made in a five-day workweek at the bank. In addition to that, everyone showered Lara with gifts. We shared rent, food and incidental expenses, but I paid for the utilities. We had plenty left over for nice meals, a full wine rack, nights out, and fresh flowers for her room and the dining table. Overall, it worked fine. But Lara had other plans for me. As soon as she started handling me, she began to change. She looked at me differently now, spoke to me differently. There was a spark in her eye, a definite glint. Her smile was always icy.

One evening before Lara left for work, she had me come to her room. She sat in her high-backed chair, which rested in the far corner of the room, facing her canopy bed. With the wave of a finger she had me on the carpet at her feet. She was wearing a black PVC dress, patent-leather heels and silky, seamless stockings. She looked remarkable. Electricity surged through me.

"How much money do you make, Mathew?" Lara asked, her magnificent ruby lips full, moist, hypnotic.

"Four hundred a week," I told her. My stomach was in a knot.

"Eyes down Mathew. Eyes on my feet. Look up only when I say you may."

I cast my eyes down as instructed.

"Very good. Now, do you have anything in the bank?"

"Yes. About four thousand, or thereabouts."

"Please refer to me as Madame, Mathew."

"Yes, Madame. Around four thousand, Madame."

I could feel her eyes looking me up and down. I had on a black shirt and a pair of loose-fitting black pants. I felt sexless in Lara's presence.

"Run along and bring me your pay stub."

I got up to get one.

"And your passbook."

"Yes, Madame."

I ran off excitedly and quickly returned with the items. I took my place again at Lara's feet, forgetting myself for a moment and looking up at her.

"Eyes down!" Lara said, berating me.

She took the pay stub and passbook and looked them over, then folded them together.

"Your pay is direct deposit?"

"Yes, Madame."

"Can it be deposited into my account?"

"I just have to give HR the pertinent information."

She was planning on taking all my money! I was swooning. With the top of her foot she pressed against my erection.

"My, my, Mathew. I see this excites you as much as it does me."

"Yes, Madame. Thank you very much."

Lara leaned forward, and with her hand under my chin, she raised my head, bringing my eyes up to meet hers.

"You're welcome, Mathew," and with that she sat back, leaving me her hand to kiss while she gave me final instructions on the matter. "Tomorrow you are to do whatever is needed to have your pay put into my account." She gave me her branch and passbook numbers. "You are to transfer your savings there as well. Do you understand?"

"Yes, Madame. I'll do it first thing in the morning."

"Good boy. And bring me back the passbook."

In supplication, I lay my head in Lara's lap. She ran her hand through my hair for a moment or two and then kissed my cheek.

"I have to go to work now, Mathew," she said delicately.

I raised my head and sat back on my heels but kept my eyes at Lara's feet.

"Madame?"

"Yes, Mathew. Not another request, I hope."

"Well, I was hoping that..." It was becoming impossible for me to ask her anything. I knew how it could upset her. But sometimes my urges were stronger than my common sense.

"Yes, Mathew, you were hoping..."

"That maybe...you could call me slave."

There. I'd said it. I reached for her hand again and kissed it.

Lara stood to leave.

"When you've proven to me you are one, Mathew," she said cooly. And with that she was gone. I knelt there for some time because I could smell her there.

I'm not sure where my need to be named slave came from. Perhaps it was just what I thought should happen. Perhaps I thought it would resolve some of the doubts that I'd been having.

A few weeks later, Lara had just gotten home from class. She was in a particularly good mood as we sat in the living room to talk.

"I'm afraid," I told her, after having

rehearsed a speech beforehand.

She seemed mildly annoyed and looked impatiently at her watch. I figured one of her lovers must be on the way over.

"What are you afraid of?" she asked.

She bent to untie her little hiking boots and pulled them off, revealing damp, dirty socks she'd worn all day. Her feet needed my attention but she pulled them away.

"Nothing in particular. I just feel like I'm being sucked into this void, like I'm disappearing."

"But you're right here. You're my slave."

She had said it! My immediate reaction was to dive at her feet and kiss them. Never had they smelled so good, and I told her so. I thanked her profusely, and though it may sound sentimental, I wept. It was because of how I had longed for this moment, how Lara had made me work for it.

But, somehow, the timing was wrong. It was as if she'd held it back until she needed it—a trump. The burst of relief I felt quickly subsided. I still felt like I was disappearing. This fear still had to be discussed. It wouldn't go away because she had finally called me her slave.

"I wanted to bring it up because sometimes my fear immobilizes me, and I didn't want you to misinterpret it."

"Look, Mathew, my feelings for you are growing every day. I was thinking that just today. This was your fantasy. You've made it mine. It's what we're doing now. Maybe someday we'll have different fantasies. Who knows?"

A sane man in my position would have accepted Lara's wisdom and zipped his lips. Instead I said, "Cassandra thinks I'm nuts."

Now Lara was upset. Cassandra was a friend of ours whom we'd met at a fetish party.

"Who the fuck is Cassandra to talk? Look how she lives her life. She fucks every hockey player that she can get her hands on. She's got no business judging anyone else's lifestyle."

"Listen, it wasn't my intent to make you mad..."

I tried thinking for a moment but my mind was mush. We went back and forth like this, until I got pissed off with Lara looking at her watch every five minutes. Inevitably, Lara had had enough. She stood up and looked at me sullenly.

"I won't have you threatening me, pulling the rug out from under us, doubting what we have. This isn't the first time. I won't have you swinging me back and forth. I've put too much into this, too much into you, for that." She hadn't raised her voice at all but she was positively fuming.

"Furthermore, Mathew, this will never happen again. Listen, and listen carefully. Our relationship is suspended, and will remain so until you've thought about what it is you want. You want to be my slave, be my slave. If not, don't. No more waffling. When you've decided, let me know. You know where to find me."

With that she stormed out of the room. Sam arrived a half hour later but they didn't stay home as usual.

I was stunned. The day she finally calls me her slave I was cut off. I felt like such an idiot. I didn't even know what I wanted any more.

THE ADVERTISEMENT FOR THE FETISH PARTY MADE me realize that I had an opportunity to find out more about the desires that hounded me, that were holding me back at the Zen centre. I thought perhaps I could resolve this conflict by indulging in my fantasies.

The days leading up to my first fetish party were hardly bearable for me. I knew that going there would change my life entirely. I had no idea what to wear, so I went to Northbound Leather and bought a pair of leather biker briefs and a matching shirt, as well as a collar and leash. I wanted to get the message across about what I was and who I was looking for. The leather clothes, heels and boots in that store were so sexy. As I strolled about the shop, I imagined who might be at the party wearing these things.

The event was held at the Lizard Lounge, a hip Church Street basement bar, where each night had a theme—women's night, men's night, fetish night. The layout was straightforward: there was a long bar at the far end of the dance floor, behind which was a separate, quiet room. There was no equipment there, just a bed at the entrance, away from the brunt of the music, a room meant for talking and erotic play. The walls were made of brown brick and the floors were concrete painted black.

This was only the second party held, but the crowd was large. It was an open party, but it had a private, underground feel to it: it was intimate and comfortable. There must have been two hundred people, maybe more. I watched the room carefully. I was awestruck by the beautiful women, their incredible outfits made of rubber, leather and metal, tight-fitting and very revealing; boots laced-up to the tops of their legs; spiky heels and fishnet stockings. Almost all of them carried toys in their hands or at their hips: riding crops, cat-o-nine tails, handcuffs. I just couldn't believe that there were so many people with whom I had this common interest. I was in heaven.

It didn't take me long to act. I saw my chance and went for it. There were a few women who had me reeling, but there was one in particular who had been hired to dance. She wore a short skirt, a halter and sheer stockings that ran down to her motorcycle boots. She was toned and fit, with a beautiful smile and long legs—a classic dancer's body. She had on a red wig. I watched her dance for almost an hour, imagining her feet getting sore and tired and steaming up inside her heavy boots. I knew her feet would love some attention and that here I could approach her. Even if she said no, I could still approach her. I knew I wouldn't be judged here. I walked calmly toward her at the end of a song.

"May I worship your feet?" I asked confidently.

She considered it for a second, looking me straight in the eye the whole time.

"Sure," she said finally.

I took her to the bed by the entrance and laid her down comfortably.

"I've never had my feet worshipped before," she told me.

Pulling off her boots was dreamlike. She was positively purring on the bed.

"No bare feet," she said. "Worship them through the stockings."

Worshipping her feet like that was painfully pleasurable. I could smell, taste and touch her, but there was still that see-through barrier of her stockings ultimately denying me.

Her name was Kay, and I would have her feet many times throughout the years. She was a tease and taunted me incessantly, which I liked. She loved my foot massages as much as I loved giving them. She often had me smell, kiss and massage her through her stockings or socks as she did that first night. "Safe Socks," the proprietor once joked while watching us.

The Lizard Lounge fetish parties were usually held once a month, becoming more frequent as time went on. Eventually another party sprang up, run by a prominent dominatrix and held at a popular dance club, the Limelight. I made up for all my lost years of frustration. I lived for fetish nights and the sexual freedom they gave me.

My thirst was insatiable. It was common for me to be with two women in a night, sometimes as many as five. Over the next eight years, I would be physically intimate on one level or another—erotic play, massage, bondage and teasing, oral penetration—with around a thousand women at these various fet nights. This was an indication of the level of my obsessive drive to satisfy my craving, to make up for what I thought I'd missed. I have always been aware of the dangers this lifestyle entails, and I have been fortuitous in this regard. With a couple of exceptions, fet nights became the only place where I was able to connect with women on the levels important to me.

For the next few weeks after Lara gave me her ultimatum, I struggled with my concerns, unable to give Lara a decision straight away. I needed time, and took it. I continued doing things for Lara that didn't infringe on her person or space—the dishes, laundry and light chores—and she again grew warm to me. We were friends living together. And while she had lover after lover after lover to our house, I took it upon myself one blizzardy December night to go to a fetish night by alone. It had been a long time.

There might have been thirty-five people there, compared with the usual two hundred and fifty, but it was fifty percent women instead of the usual fifteen percent. One of them was Claudia, a lovely nineteen year old who had strolled over from her mother's home across the street. What else was a young woman to do on a stormy Canadian winter night?

She told me she was born in Uruguay, of Spanish heritage, and had moved to Canada at a young age. She spoke five languages—Italian, Portuguese, Spanish, French and English. She was bright, fresh and sexy and had an infectious laugh. We sat at the bar together all night and danced a little, too. She had on black leather shorts that laced up the sides, a leather vest and Dr. Martens boots. Her hair was long, golden and braided.

She came home with me after the party. Lara wasn't there. We went straight to my room, where we flipped through a photo album of mine and just talked. She grew sleepy as did I, and I helped her undress and go to bed. We simply slept side by side, nothing more. When I woke, she was sleeping softly in the pale winter's light. I marvelled at Claudia as she lay asleep, and ran my finger along the smooth lines of her figure. How could anything be so beautiful in nineteen short years?

Eventually Claudia woke up, too. Lara still wasn't home. She had had countless lovers, and yet there I was feeling guilty for no reason other than having met a friend. Claudia and I had breakfast before I walked her to the subway. I knew I had met someone who would be a close friend for years to come.

I lit a fire and sat in the living room waiting for Lara to come home. I thought about all the women I had met at fetish parties, as well as the women from outside of that world that I had tried to connect with. I thought of the friends I knew who had never lived their dreams, who were still trapped in a world of make-believe and shadows. Desires as strong as mine cannot be ignored, I concluded. There had been a thousand women, a thousand pairs of feet, innumerable interactions; but rather than variety, it had been the same relatively shallow experience over and over again. I could not pass up the opportunity to go deep with my dream. I had nothing to lose. I was determined to give myself to Lara once and for all.

It had long been my dream to have a Mistress, one woman to whom I would devote myself, one woman who would own and control me in every way.

      Dominant women usually have the role of top introduced to them later in life. The most common characteristic of most female doms, in my experience, is a general lack of respect for men, due to abuse as a child, rape or other difficulties relating to men. Conversely, my vision of my Mistress was of a woman with a childlike innocence and a pure beauty. My Mistress would be firm in her word and expectations, and in her training of me, yet ultimately loving, respectful of my place at her feet, affectionate and devoted to me as much as I would be to her. I would be almost like her dog, I suppose. In this way, the slave is always the Mistress' mainstay, no matter how many lovers she takes, no matter what she does with her time or where she goes. She always has her slave as a constant, a person who is there for her, obedient, worshipful, attentive. The Mistress therefore rewards her slave with love, affection and the kind of attention he craves so much: to be taken, handled, utilized, wrung for everything he's worth.

My fantasy Mistress wouldn't have to go out of her way to handle me. It would be as much her passion as it was mine. In this manner, lustful, dominant women excited me. I could imagine them thrusting their demands upon me, using that desire to love, not hate, me.

The fantasy was lifelong, intense and grew with my experiences at fetish nights, mainly because those experiences weren't so much real as they were extensions of my fantasy.

In the space of one evening at a fet night, a woman could be whatever I wished her to be. I didn't know her, so no interaction with her or thought of her could get in the way of what I saw, of what I pretended she was to me. And she didn't know me either, so there was no time for me to do or say anything for her to act upon. The woman, her personality and her heart, mattered to me, but it was because I didn't know her that I was able to imagine she was what I wanted and needed.

Yet, it was rare that I would find myself with the same woman more than once. If I got to know her after erotic play, the fantasy rarely remained intact. For one reason or another the fantasy bubble would pop. Over time this repetition became empty and meaningless to me. The physical interaction was real but the mental interaction—the most important aspect of the Mistress/slave relationship—was not. It was only fantasy: two people projecting ideals onto each other. As a consequence of my growing dissatisfaction with my role in the scene, I fervently began seeking out my Mistress. It would be almost as intangible a search as my spiritual one.

After I had decided to go deep with my dream, the Mistress/slave relationship between Lara and I did grow and evolve. Over the next few months, a feeling of contentment came back to me. I counted my blessings. As time passed, I trusted Lara more. In the first year and a half of our relationship, I had tortured myself by imagining our troubles were rooted in some ulterior motive of hers; after all, I was in quite a vulnerable position with Lara. But despite my overall satisfaction with the progress of our relationship, there was one aspect of it that continued to founder: our physical intimacy as Mistress and slave. I knew Lara preferred women sexually but there were many ways we could have approached this issue. She had said to me more than once that if I wanted something, I should beg for it rather than whine or complain, so I decided to bring up this issue differently than anything I'd ever brought up before.

It was pretty late, and Lara had just arrived home from work. I wanted so badly to have her feet, which she'd been on all night. I could imagine them, their smell, taste and texture, but she had met someone at the bar who was on her way over. I knelt before her while she sat in the armchair in her room. She kicked off her heels, revealing her lovely, tired soles.

"May I worship your feet, Madame?" I had on my best puppy-dog face.

"Not tonight, Mathew. I'm expecting someone any minute."

She seemed a bit annoyed with me. How could I be an inconvenience?

"I'm sorry, Madame. You told me to beg for things, so I am, even though it doesn't tend to get me anywhere—"

"Mathew. You get my feet when I say you can have them. Not otherwise. You're the slave, remember?"

"It's just that you're always saying 'later' but later almost never comes."

Of course, Lara could remember a dozen times she had granted me my wishes, but over the course of the past two years, it was sparse at best. She sat regally in her chair, elegant and beautiful, driving me mad with lust.

"Mathew, I appreciate your frustration. It's something I enjoy very much," she said with a sly smile. "You're not patient enough. If you got everything you wanted all at once, you wouldn't be happy either. It's a fine balance, one that I must find. Mathew…you must be patient."

"Forgive me, Madame, it's just that some times I feel like I'll be waiting forever. You spend so much time with your lovers because I do all the work here so you don't have to. Couldn't you spend more time with me? I'm begging you. It's killing me."

"Mathew, I didn't want to say anything. As you know, I like things to take their course. Mystery can be good. But I've only ever been with one man and have only ever been close with two others. All things are possible with us as Mistress and slave. You must be patient. It can only happen if and when I say. And Mathew," she waved a finger at me, "you are my slave. You exist to obey me, perform for me, worship me and support me. You are so very fortunate to be kneeling here now."

Those words should have eased my mind, but they didn't. I said no more and decided to heed her words, but there was something unsettled in me, some great doubt.

It was in me like rot in wood. Still, my lustful needs won out again—I'd waited so long, given up so much, had nowhere else to go.

Why do I need this? I asked myself. *Why do I like this even though it tortures me? Mathew, Lara's slave. Is this who I am?* A mystic master once said, "Until you have lain awake all night, unable to swallow even a crumb, you will not find the answer." I knew exactly what he meant.

"May I at least kiss your feet before I go?" I begged once again.

Lara brought one leg up and rested her foot on my shoulder, and brought her other foot against my crotch, causing my chastity device to rise and swell with me. She smiled with her eyes.

"No, Mathew, you may not kiss my feet." And with that she put them to my face, rubbed them over me, letting me smell her, letting me feel her wetness through the damnable barrier of her stocking.

When she was finished with me, she withdrew her precious feet and said, "Go to your room and dream of me, Mathew—and remember how fortunate you are."

I began to rise but she pushed me down as she stood.

"Crawl, Mathew. You will not leave the

floor in my presence, unless granted permission," she said, smiling. She was pleased with that one.

"Now leave me, Mathew."

I crawled to my bed only to toss and turn between graphic dreams of worshipping and loving my Mistress and the sounds of her incessant lovemaking that went on till morning. When did she sleep?

Lara thrilled in her dominion over me. It amazed her what she could have me do, the hoops she could have me jump through. She told me once that she had fantasies of seeing just how far she could take me. I didn't know what she meant. I'd heard of a slave castrated by his Mistress, and of a man and woman who were so masochistic they confessed to a crime and went to jail so that their Mistress could get off with the money. I figured Lara's comment was just an offhand remark. I wouldn't take it seriously until later.

Lara had difficulty finding punishments for me that didn't deny her, too. Once, while hand-washing some of her clothes, I inadvertently hung two dresses near enough to each other that colours ran from the black to the red. My punishment? She took me to a fetish night and had me massage the feet of the least attractive transvestite she could find. Unfortunately for Lara, I actually enjoyed it because she was so happy with herself and her wicked mind.

I bought matching dye and made the spotted dress look as good as new, or so I thought. In daylight it looked fine, but under club lighting all the splotches showed up clearly. Lara didn't find out until she got to work. I thought it was funny. It would make a good comedy to have a slave stumbling around his Mistress, spilling drinks and food on her, over-starching her linen, screwing up in general. Lara didn't think it was so funny.

She told me of other punishments she had for me, like finding people who would pay to have sex with me (she would give the money to her lovers), or forcing me to perform oral sex on a women she knew I found distasteful, or buying a pet pig, attaching blinking lights to it and making me walk it through the neighbourhood. She was creative, my Mistress. She put fear into me, and at times I dreaded the extent and outcome of her power.

"Oh, I know you're not ready for anything like that, Mathew," Lara said of her cruel threats. "But I can make you ready."

I knew she could, but she would have to take steps she'd been unwilling to take till then.

As each fetish party came and went, I longed for the next, my fantasies of finding a Mistress growing stronger all the while. As I became more and more entwined in the fetish scene, my attention and energy shifted away from my Zen practices. The conflict I felt between these two worlds held me back both spiritually and sexually, I felt that I had to choose one or the other. So, despite my problems with the practices at the Zen centre, I tried to immerse myself in *zazen* again, hoping to find insight through the practices, to find out who I really was and where I belonged.

  Zen Buddhism for me is not so much a religion as it is a formal, structured questioning that has been passed down from sages. I say this because once the answers start coming, you learn to stand on your own feet. *Zazen* is a way of focusing the mind, a way of penetrating past thought to what lays beyond, to experience the organic experience of Oneness. In *Rinzai* Zen, *zazen* is usually a classically paradoxical koan, one that can come naturally or can be assigned, such as *What is it?* or *Who am I?* or *What is the sound of one hand clapping?* For many people, even the breathing discipline of *Soto* Zen awareness practice alone has opened up questions for them, such as *Why is there so much suffering in the world?* or *Is there a God?* or *Is there a purpose to all this?* There are answers to these questions, inward and outward confirmations that come, not from the discriminating intellect, but from direct experience and insight into the one secret of the universe. Zen Buddhists, Catholic contemplatives, Muslim Suffis and all other true mystic paths deal directly with these questions and answers, and the method of their practice takes practitioners to this direct experience.

There were distinct similarities between my Zen and fetish interests. Something in me needed to be controlled. Zen has a master; I longed for a Mistress. *Zazen* requires the practitioner to assume a motionless, traditional posture surrender himself to meditation; my Mistress demanded the complete surrender of my will, and could immobilize me at her whim. The *zendo* master holds the long energizing stick during formal sitting; my Mistress carries her whip. Zen and sado-masochism were the closest things to my heart. All my friends were from one life or the other. But whether either of these lifestyles trapped or freed me was still unclear.

Behind all of this there was an answer, but I didn't know if I even knew the right question. I was beginning to question whether the Zen centre was even the right place for me to search for my answers. The koan my *sensei* assigned me was *What is mu?*, which is a fairly standard initial question that means *What is nothing?* This koan was different from the ones that had occurred to me naturally, *What am I? What is this?*, and I repelled it internally. The patriarchal and hierarchal structure of the lineage of the temple was not consistent with the Buddhist concept of Oneness; all is One and any concepts of separateness are illusory.

Furthermore, when I tried to meditate, all I thought of was my fantasy Mistress, of her doing to me all the things I longed for. In such situations, my *sensei* instructed me to let go, to focus on my meditation, but the pull was too strong. The spirit needs to let go, the body needs to hold on. My affinity with Zen and meditation was based on a need for truth, clarity and simplification. My love for s/m, my need for a submissive relationship, was lustful, material and physical. I had to explore this conflict freely and my first step was to leave the Zen centre, to take the plunge and pursue my natural koan, to see if fetish was who I really was.

It was 8 p.m. when Lara got home with Sam. They'd had a pint or two at the pub around the corner and wanted me to come out and join them. It was the first time I'd gone anywhere with Lara and Sam, besides fetish nights. We each had a couple of pints before going back home. It was a nice time. I felt we were becoming like a family, albeit a strange one.

We sat around the living room, listening to music and chatting. At some point I noticed Sam and I were alone and had been for nearly half an hour. I asked Sam where Lara had gone. She shrugged and smiled. Ten minutes later Lara walked down the stairs, wearing a tight leather miniskirt and the most gorgeous, thigh-high leather boots I'd ever seen. When she got to the last stair, I got a good look. She was stunning. She had on a biker jacket and under that, nothing but one of her beautiful satin bras.

She had a crop in her hand and a gleam in her eye.

"Mathew," she said in her silken voice, "take off your clothes and crawl to my room."

I gawped at Lara, unable to move for a second. I began to disrobe and felt awkward, sexless, as I often did in Lara's presence.

"Fold your things and leave them stacked neatly on the chair," she instructed.

"Yes, Madame."

My heart was pounding. Was my fantasy becoming a reality? It all seemed far away, like it was happening to someone else and I was just watching it pass by. I crawled up the stairs and into her room where she handcuffed me, kneeling and blindfolded, to the foot of her bed.

I could hear Lara and Sam talking behind me. Sam left the room. Momentarily, Melissa Etheridge's "Precious Pain" began playing on Lara's stereo. Suddenly, Lara brought a thick belt down on me, connecting just below my tailbone. I writhed in agony, straining against the cuffs.

I thought *lower* and Lara said, "I know. It felt too high. But it was right where I wanted it."

No form of physical contact or sex, before or since, has moved me as Lara did that night with the attentiveness of her whip. I wept openly. I purged. I cried out my love for her. I begged for her love and understanding, all while she worked me over, top to bottom, then over again, a beautiful pain washing over me.

    Lara took off her jacket and the blindfold long enough for me to see her perfectly-formed breasts pushed up and out by her lovely bra. I winced at the sight of her and Lara laughed, a metallic, almost mechanical laugh that chilled my spine. Then she returned to the task at hand and whipped me so long and hard I swore I could feel blood dripping down my backside. In reality, through the corner of the blindfold, I caught sight of Lara in one of the mirrors as she squirted water over me now and again.

    I'd never been whipped much before. Whipping is a classic interaction that tells the slave he belongs to his Mistress, that she may use him as she pleases, for punishment or on a whim. Nevertheless, it wasn't my thing, even though I felt that the spirit of a Mistress/slave relationship dictated such things take place, that they were instrumental in forming a lasting bond.

    I had seen many whippings. Usually the top, or dominatrix, starts gently, builds slowly and crescendos to a pleasurable peak. Not Lara. Full tilt all the way. My Zen training came in handy here. I put myself into the pain, became the pain, so that it was no longer something separate that could be hated or resented. There was no Lara, no me, no whip; just whipping.

Eventually, though, it became too much for me to handle physically, and I began to flinch and squirm away from Lara and her touch. She kept on and on, with no respite. I started to lose my composure, my focus. I started to wonder if she was loving me or hating me. I collapsed.

I believe Lara would have gone on and on had Sam not walked in. Sam stopped Lara, and bent down and held me firmly. My body was convulsing and repelled her touch, too. Sam spoke calmly and reassuringly, and eventually I calmed down. She unlocked the handcuffs, which were all that kept me from falling down altogether. I fell to a heap and rested there until I could gather myself.

"Too bad," Lara said to me. It was as if her voice emanated from inside my own brain. "I was going to let you watch us tonight."

All I saw was her carpet. Sam was helping me to my hands and knees.

"He's all right," Lara told Sam. "Mathew, crawl to your room. I'll see you there shortly."

Slowly I moved in that direction. I got to my futon and gently rolled onto it. Through it all I was fully erect. Thank God I hadn't been wearing the chastity belt during the whipping.

Lying there was difficult. I itched all over and was in no shape to shower, which wold have only made it worse anyway. Lying on my side was bearable. I rested, slowly caught my breath and waited for Lara.

I could not have bought Lara's whipping in a million years. For me, it was something that had to be bestowed. Yet, like all things, it had come and gone. At once I felt an overwhelming completeness and a hollow emptiness. I waited for Lara. I couldn't sleep. I gingerly rolled onto my other side.

At last she strutted in, barefoot, triumphant. She bent over me and stuffed one of the stockings she'd been wearing into my mouth. The other she slipped over my penis and cinched around my balls. Then she tied my wrists together over my head to my bed frame. I could only look up at her in rapture.

"Contemplate how fortunate you are to taste me, Mathew, how fortunate you are to be mine."

From heaven to hell, and back again, all within my thoughts. I was reminded of the samurai who approached a Zen master and asked him about heaven and hell.

"I'd tell you," the master said, "but it wouldn't do any good."

"Why not?" wondered the samurai.

The master looked him up and down.

"Because you look daft. You wouldn't understand."

"How dare you," the samurai screamed. He was enraged, and unsheathed his sword and raised it over his head to strike.

"There!" said the master. "That is hell."

With that the samurai lowered his sword in supplication.

"And that," said the master, "is heaven."

Lara had me on my full workload the very next day; it was as if nothing had changed. She showed me off to a few of her friends, pointing out the purple-and-black welts and counting the seventeen places where she'd broken my skin.

"It was awesome," she said. "I'd always wanted to whip Mathew."

Alcohol had been an element of Lara's whipping me, and when I thought about it, it bothered me. But I let it go. There was good reason to think that in the long run everything would work out. I had thought about saying something, but our gears ground when it came to communicating. Lara believed that things should just happen, whereas I felt that knowing one another through communication allowed deeper, more honest events to unfold. Besides, if it took a few beer, so what? Her approach was agonizing, but I had to admit that she was taking me beyond my fantasies. Moreover, around this time she began to refer to me often as her slave, even in front of people who had no business knowing. She didn't care. It was her life.

Lara paid extra attention now to my work and its completeness. She demanded perfection. She noticed the slightest spot on her bathroom faucet or a bad crease in something I'd pressed. Even as her slave it amazed me how one woman could put a man to work all day, every day. She even suggested in one of her offhand remarks that she wanted me to get a second job, to bring her more money.

This was the third year of our relationship. There was again great simplicity for me, and it was a soft, quiet time for us. All I had to do was obey her. Everything I did was for her, except that in doing so, I was also fulfilling my own desires. I had no worries or anxieties then, no bills to pay—nothing to do but do as I was told. Lara, on the other hand, had all the responsibility and decisions to make that came along with the benefits of being Mistress.

I didn't even have to concern myself with clothes. Lara outfitted me. I had a small mix-and-match wardrobe for work, a few regular clothes and a uniform, a sort of fetish butler's outfit that I was to wear while serving around the house. The jacket had an exquisite cut, and the pants were tight and stretchy, and she had a dozen bow ties in a variety of colours for me to wear. Lara got a real kick out of it. "I'd get bored with you in black all day," she said to me.

My services were still mostly domestic but a few new tasks or privileges had been added. Lara brought cookbooks home for me, and soon I was cooking and serving all her meals. She positively adored running me off my feet. She would sit at the dinner table relaxing while I ran about, sweat dripping from my brow, pouring this, fetching that. I loved her for it. When she had company, I ate after she had eaten and all the dishes were done. When we were alone, she would often let me eat on the floor, at her feet. She loved me at her feet and she would purr whenever I was there.

Lara liked to leash me around the house and at fetish parties. She taught me to heel and with a few subtle signals could have me sit, kneel, massage her feet, whatever. She liked me to do what she wanted me to do with the least amount of effort on her part. She wanted me to be an extension of her thoughts, to anticipate her needs as much as possible. This excited me very much and I worked very hard to please her.

I had tried to let go of some of our unresolved issues, too, and decided to let things be. I loved Lara completely, and even though she had many issues with men and relationships, I felt a great deal of love coming from her, too. Most importantly, Lara was happy with me now and who knew what that might bring?

In spite of all this wonderful attention, there was an element of insincerity to it, as in the past, as if she was doing solely as a way to attain her own ends. I don't know how much of this was paranoia on my part, but she knew that she needed to give in order to get. She really had me then, even though she actually spent almost no time with me. She was too busy with her lovers.

Our moments together came before her lovers arrived, or before she left for work. I spent a lot of time in our home alone, washing this, ironing that. I wondered if this was the simplicity that I longed for. It hadn't been so simple getting here, and there were no guarantees it would last. I tried not to think about things too much, but even in the midst of it, my fantasy seemed to be passing me by. It didn't make sense.

Every so often that icy curtain fell over Lara's eyes. I noticed it only as she used her power over me more and more. Power excited her sexually and this realization both thrilled and frightened her. Like my need to be at her feet, her need to have me there became overwhelming. She terrified and excited me when she got like that.

One evening, Lara was lying on her bed, trance-like. We were alone. None of her lovers were coming over. I lay there with her.

"This room is too crowded," she said, looking straight up at the ceiling.

In addition to her canopy bed there were four chests of drawers, her armchair and two glass sculptures.

"I need to get this shit out of here. I was looking through an *Architectural Digest* and they showed a bedroom with just the bed. It was awesome."

"I've got lots of space in my room," I said. "Move it in there, I don't mind."

She thought for a moment, her cool calculation palpable.

"That's no good. I don't want you there every time I need something. I need a bedroom and a dressing room."

"We could get a bigger place," I suggested. "You seem to be making good money."

She was making a lot of money at the bar, but I didn't ask how much.

"No, I like it here," she said, shaking her head. "I don't think you could withstand the work of another move."

"There's always my room, then." I blurted out.

Lara thought for a moment. A smile worked its way over her lips.

"Yes, Mathew," she said at last, "there is. Tomorrow I want you to clean out your room and move your stuff downstairs."

Downstairs was the basement, a small, unfinished, cement room with a furnace, water heater and a hundred boxes full of Lara's things.

"Clean the room thoroughly," she went on, "and move my things in. Make sure this room is cleaned well, too. And I want more mirrors up. They'll have to be rearranged."

"Yes, Madame."

Lara looked away from the ceiling and at me. She smiled beautifully before looking away, losing herself in thought.

Few and far between, moments like those were what I lived for. For all my complaining and whining, only Lara could deliver what I wanted.

"Make sure you're out of the way down there," Lara said. "Put the top of your bed frame near the support pole at the far end so I can shackle you there."

"I will, Madame."

Lara, annoyed, looked over at me and said, "Mathew, aren't you going to thank me?"

"Yes, Madame. Thank you for your kind consideration and for the opportunity to serve and please you." I was absolutely gushing.

Lara lay there in her blue-and-white satin wrap, happy as can be.

"Mathew, hand me my phone."

Deflated, I reached for it. She made me dial Sam's number. While waiting for Sam to answer she said, "Mathew, you may have my feet if you want."

Did I ever.

Lara began chaining me to my bed whenever I wasn't in use. There were times I thought she'd forget me entirely, but that was silly. It gave me opportunity for reflection, lying there with nothing else to do.

My life seemed unreal, even surreal. I'd dreamed of being chained up at my Mistress' mercy, yet actually being there was strangely sexless and unexciting. It shouldn't have surprised me—it wasn't the first time it had happened. I had to lie to myself to complete the fantasy. I told myself, "This is where I need to be." I told myself, "Lara loves me" I told myself, "You have nothing to lose." I couldn't back out.

The doubt never left me though; it was my shadow. I had pangs of remorse when I thought what certain friends and family members would think if they knew how I lived my life, if they could have seen me. Could I live an entire life as Lara's slave without anyone ever knowing? Lara wanted everyone to know—in her own time. Should I care what anyone would think?

Another fear that began to eat away at me was what if Lara got bored with me?

"I was thinking of getting you another job," she said to me again. "I could get another slave to pick up the slack around here." She wasn't serious, but she wasn't kidding either. She was testing me.

"If what we have is solid, there's nothing you can't wring from me," I said truthfully. I no longer thought that what we had was solid. Her life was her lovers. But a Mistress can get a slave to do whatever she wants, in time, if she's willing to make sacrifices herself .

I was becoming less and less willing to be

pushed further towards the edge. I needed more of the physical closeness Lara denied me. I believe Lara wanted to push me as far as possible. She said something once about her ultimate achievement. It would be for me to serve and worship without even ever seeing her, let alone touching her. She had me construct an alter to her worship, which had, among other things, photos of her and recently worn stockings and underthings. This drove me mad, with anger or lust—I was never sure which.

I HAD MADE A LOT OF GOOD FRIENDS OVER THE FIVE years that I had been involved in Zen and fetish. Over the three years I had spent with Lara I'd neglected them. I knew my friends understood, and some of them were even envious of my position with Lara. I was lucky. I was young enough, confident enough, and had the right looks to pull it off, to get what I wanted. Some of my friends weren't so fortunate. One of them, Joel, was in his late fifties. He had left the fetish life in New York when he was in his early twenties, to pursue a normal life with a wife and kids. It would have been a lot harder to live my lifestyle when he was young because there was no community, almost no literature, no understanding. He somewhat regretted this aspect of his life and was trying desperately to make up for lost time. Unfortunately, many dominant women aren't interested in older submissive men when there are so many young ones about.

Another friend, in a desperate attempt to keep his Mistress, who was a pro and had many subs, sold his business and gave her the money. When I had last seen him, he was alone and working as a labourer. She had just moved into a new home in a trendy area.

Desperadoes is what we called them. I knew I was becoming one.

I HAD BEEN ASKING A LOT OF QUESTIONS, PROBABLY because of my jealousy and frustration with Lara's lovers, as if knowing the answers would help. Sam and I had been getting to know one another and Lara didn't like that. She thought if we put our heads together we might figure her out.

"She loves you," Sam reassured me one morning over coffee. Lara was getting ready upstairs. "You have your hands on her most intimate things. She doesn't trust any of us that far."

I knew this, but the situation was complex and I had recurring difficulty dealing with it. Sam's caring words helped tremendously.

It turned out she knew about two of Lara's lovers. I told Sam she was Lara's favourite by far, and she was. She was over as much as all the others combined. Sam knew what was going on, and my comments helped, but she took this confirmation hard.

Lara could not have seen a friendship between Sam and me as benefiting her. I never meant to betray Lara, but I had no outlet, no one to talk to. I was only trying to find answers for myself. Sam and I also had in common our deep affection for Lara.

Sam often went with us to fet nights, or I should say I often went with Lara and Sam. We always had fun when we went out, but I was always playing second fiddle. Yet there I was. This time I soon became bored sitting by Lara while she and Sam got it on, so I asked if I could walk around to see if I could find anyone I knew.

Cruising the club that night showed me that even though Lara was my Mistress and my love, I still lusted after feet, even those of other women. For a while I thought I wasn't interested in any one else, but this night showed me the plain facts of my fetish. I don't think I could ever have had enough feet: you could have lined up enough women to circle three times around the globe, and it still wouldn't have been enough. It was now one more thing to drive me nuts—all those off-limits feet walking around. It wasn't just feet, either. My tongue was itching for something, anything, to do.

When I got back to our table, I was crushed—there was Sam with Lara's feet. There was nothing I could say. What I had with Lara fit into such a small box that I wasn't willing to share it. Sam had all of her. Hurt, I stormed off. Lara called to me and I ignored her. Big mistake.

I found a dark corner and hid there to gather myself. I was never a match for Lara. She always had a way with words or actions that soundly defeated anything I could come up with.

Lara was furious and wasted no time finding me. She has no concern at all for how I feel, I remember thinking as she confronted me. Her concern was herself. She reamed me out right there in the club, and it was no Mistress/slave thing. I'd seen her yell like that twice, once at Sam and another time at one of her other lovers. I couldn't stand her yelling at me. I got my things from the coat check and went home.

A few hours later I heard Sam and Lara come in and go to her room. I could hear them having sex through the vent. It kept me up all night, as usual. But when I heard the whip, my spirit broke. I slept the sleep of the dead. When I woke, I wondered if I even loved Lara or if it was the Mistress of my fantasy that I loved.

One Saturday night a few weeks later when Lara was out with Sam, friends of ours, Martin and Joanne, stopped by unexpectedly to see us. I asked them in and we ended up around the dining room table drinking Lara's wine. It was a thoroughly enjoyable night for me. I realized then how tight my life was. Letting loose felt good. It was exhilarating to talk and laugh under normal circumstances, and it was comfortable because Martin and Joanne knew about Lara and me. Time flowed quickly that night, as did Lara's wine.

  Around one in the morning, Lara came home. She was happy to see her friends and me in a jovial mood. Sam came in and they sat with us. Eventually Lara's eyes darted from me to the empty wine bottles and back again.

  "Mathew's been really funny," Martin told Lara.

  "He doesn't get out much," was her response. She looked at me without smiling. A shiver went down my spine.

  "I admit, I was on," I offered.

  "Where'd the wine come from?" Lara asked, looking directly at me.

  "From the rack," I answered. "I thought it would be rude not to offer Martin and Joanne some wine."

"Of course you did, Mathew," she said sarcastically.

Martin and Joanne exchanged uncomfortable glances.

"We were just having a little fun," I said. "And there's plenty of wine left."

"We'll talk about it tomorrow, Mathew. Say good night."

I accepted Lara bumming me out, but she didn't have to ruin everyone else's night. I said good night and stood up to leave.

"On second thought," Lara thought for a moment. "Mathew, pull your pants down."

Out of the blue, just like that. I wasn't sure I'd heard her correctly but I dropped my pants anyway, in case I had. Lara brought me to the stairwell and leaned me over the railing.

She had on jeans, a red leather jacket and matching cowboy boots. She was wearing a thick, studded, red leather belt. With a loud *zip* Lara pulled the belt out.

"A dozen lashes for each bottle, Mathew. How many lashes is that?"

I was shaking and unable to vocalize.

"What was that Mathew? I can't hear you."

"Two dozen lashes, Madame. Thank you."

Lara walked calmly back and forth behind me.

"I want you to count them out loud, Mathew, and I want you to thank me after each one."

I dared a glance back.

"No, Mathew. Look straight ahead. No whining either. Just counting and thankfulness."

"Yes, Madame."

What could Joanna and Martin have been thinking?

Lara put everything into each stroke. After every other stroke she would sip some wine and make a deprecating comment about my ass or about my whining. She followed through hard with each stroke. I could barely stand it. The twelfth stroke sent me to my knees.

"UP, MATHEW!" Lara screamed. "You're embarrassing me in front of my friends."

"You trained me," I managed to say, foolishly. Maybe it was the wine talking.

The others laughed at that. Lara swiftly awarded an additional dozen lashes for my comment. It was as if she'd anticipated my remark.

With each stroke I yelled out the required count and thanks. A dozen strokes left and it was no longer funny to anyone. Lara had a knack for that. Again I wondered what her motive was, love or hate? One stroke was particularly hard to take: a portion of her belt had a great deal of metal on it and it struck my tailbone.

"Suck it up, Mathew." That was Lara's response as I writhed in horrible agony. "Compliment me on my aim."

"Impeccable as always," I said, through clenched teeth.

The thirty-fifth stroke sent me to the carpet, for good.

"One more Mathew. Get up." There was no softness in her voice.

I moved toward her boot to kiss it. She flinched away. I hated her then. I couldn't stand the thought of one more lash from her. All I felt was hostility and repulsion towards her, but I counted the last stroke, given to me as I lay before her, and thanked her, too. I rolled to my back and looked up at her. The curtain that had dropped over Lara's eyes as she gave me the beating had risen again. She was jovial and even allowed me up and to sit with them and drink more wine. I had thought my punishment was over.

Lara spent the night and all day Sunday with Sam. Whomever she was with, it wasn't me. I went to work on Monday and came home at lunch to retrieve an item for a co-worker. Lara was home. It was the first time since Saturday evening's beating that I'd seen her.

Lara was still steaming about the liberties I'd taken with the wine. She was in the kitchen sitting with a coffee, wearing her satin wrap, and of course, her heels. The wrap fell just below her hips, grazing the tops of her thighs, revealing her incredibly smooth, tan legs as she sat cross-legged.

"Kneel," she demanded, and when I did, she began a tirade that took me completely off guard. Her anger swirled like a twister. She brought up every mistake I'd ever made. An outsider would have thought it ridiculous, even comical, but for me it was sheer hell. As long as I wanted her, as long as I wanted a Mistress, I was truly helpless.

"Please forgive me," I begged, my heart pounding, fear overtaking me. "We all make mistakes. It's what we do about it that counts."

Nothing I said mattered to her.

"You have no respect for me, Mathew. You treat me as if I'm nothing to you."

I could have said the same thing to her.

"Everything is going so well," I pleaded. "All I did was have wine with your friends. You punished me already. What more do you want?"

I could take little more of Lara's hostility.

"I love being your slave," I told her. "I love you." But as I said the words I asked myself, do I?

I had to get back to work so Lara released me, but she was still in an irrational rage when I left. The streetcar ride to work was hazy as my mind tried to make sense of it all.
My doubt and fear gripped me. Somehow I made it to the blue-grey steel tower on Bay Street.

I got through the first set of security doors and then I lost it. I got through the next set of doors and wound around the corner to the coat check. Someone there saw me and told my co-worker, Loni, a good friend of many years. She had even been to a fetish night and had met Lara, but didn't know many details. I sat down, head in hands, and began trembling, trying so hard to keep my weeping from turning into wailing. Loni held me and spoke reassuringly to me. She knew instinctively what was wrong. She had said many times that Lara was no good for me and that I could do better. Loni calmed me down, enough so that she was able to get me up and out of there, and down to the food court.

It was not Loni's intention to solve my problem, but to have me settle down so I could get home and deal with Lara. Loni had always been an intelligent, insightful friend. She knew me inside out, accepted all of me.

Why can't I love you like I love Lara? I thought while hugging her goodbye. *Why can't I love someone who'll understand and appreciate me?*

I left for home feeling much better but still shaky. My skin was cool and clammy. I prayed Lara was gone. She wasn't.

When I stepped in the door I was in no mood to see or talk to Lara, but she was sitting in the living room and I had to pass her to get to my room downstairs. I glanced at her as I stepped past. I felt nothing, not fear, anger, love—nothing. She seemed happier, friendlier now. It was as if she were an actress in a movie and not real at all.

"I called you at work. They said you were coming home," she called out.

I continued past and started down the stairs but stopped there out of politeness.

"I'm sorry," she said

I just stood there, not looking at her.

"Are you okay?"

I had nothing to say and couldn't have said it if I had.

"You'll feel better after a nap," she said. It was all rambling to me. "And I've been thinking. You do work hard around here, Mathew. I think a reward is due."

Only when she has to is all that came to my mind. I slept like a zombie until the next morning, and when I woke up, I was never happier that I had work to go to, a place where I could be far away from Lara.

The wielding and yielding of control exists to some degree in any relationship. It can be agreed upon, open and healthy, or it can be manipulative. Dom/sub relationships have always impressed me with their potential for honesty; but they are also vulnerable to the worst kind of manipulation and degradation. It seemed to me that my relationship with Lara had gone down that path.

It had taken me a long time to connect with a woman in the scene, mostly because my only connection with the women I met there was sex and fetish. When I considered some of the healthier relationships I witnessed in the fet world, my difficulty with having a lasting relationship in the scene made sense to me. Most of the emotionally healthy couples there had met outside the scene and had come into it together. They usually partook in play from time to time, but it wasn't a lifestyle. More importantly, it wasn't the only thing that held them together.

Sub men are a complex lot. In general, they are desperate. I know I was. The reason for this, I believe, is that their desires have become so precise as a result of fantasizing from childhood that they become boxed in by their ideals, and have little chance of meeting someone who can fit in that box with them. Then out of frustration they lower their expectations to fulfill their needs and get screwed over, time and again.

So I began facing myself, my own desires, compulsions and motives. My fantasy had always been to be slave to a beautiful, dominant woman. I now had exactly that and yet I wasn't happy. I couldn't go on like this. The supposed joys were empty of any real, lasting happiness. What I felt while fantasizing and what I felt while experiencing many of the fantasies was completely different. It depressed me that reality was not like fantasy. It all seemed fake to me.

Motive was the key to understanding Lara's relationship with me, how she felt about me as a person and as her slave. Sam told me that Lara had been severely abused as a child and then kicked out of her step-father's home, all before she was twelve. She and her siblings had to steal food and clothes at times. Sam tried to get her to look into these things with a therapist. Lara wouldn't have it. It was clear that she disliked or at least mistrusted men. It seemed that she wanted to love them. Though she called herself a lesbian she wasn't really, she was bisexual. Lara was eventually drawn to me because as a slave I was less threatening. She was in control. An element of child abuse, of course, is the child's lack of control over adults' actions, especially the ones they rely on for food and shelter.

    Lara always had to be in control with her lovers. Over the years she had developed sophisticated ways of maneuvering them because she was deathly afraid of losing her grip. I couldn't blame her for her self-protective mechanisms. She had been through things that I couldn't begin to relate to. However, she was making no attempt at change. She let herself be guided by her old fears and experiences.

    After speaking with Sam I decided that Lara's controlling nature and her mistrust and perhaps hatred of men was what I was experiencing as her slave. She didn't have much respect for me, I had felt this even early on in our relationship. Maybe her hatred of men had led her to women. I don't know. Ninety-nine percent of Lara was beautiful, intelligent, thoughtful, but the one percent that was cold ran straight through her.

Lara was living in the fast lane. She was drinking and partying a lot, and there was a period of a couple of weeks when neither Sam nor I saw much of Lara. I knew she couldn't be alone because she was never alone. But where was she spending her time? Who was she with? One morning, I woke around three to use the washroom, passing Lara's room along the way. Mystery solved. I knew I had to talk to someone, so I called Sam from a pay phone down the street.

"What's up?" Sam asked after I excitedly told her it was me.

"She'll kill me for talking to you," I began, "but I have to talk about it and you're the only one."

"Take it easy, Mathew. What is it?"

I can't say whether I trusted Sam or not. She was generally good-hearted, but she was also not beyond doing or saying what she had to in order to get what she wanted. At least this is how she was with Lara. I believe she felt she could trust me and was no longer threatened by me.

"Lara had a guy last night."

There was dead silence on Sam's end. I could barely believe the words as I said them aloud.

"I knew it," Sam said finally. "She meets all kinds of guys at work. It was bound to happen."

Sam was devastated, I could sense it through the wires.

"I can't stay here," I said.

"Calm down, Mathew."

"I know what she'll say, too. That it's her business. Technically she thinks she's justified—"

"Like she always is."

"I'm gonna snap. She just does what she wants and fuck anyone else."

"She's a troubled gal," Sam said. "I've tried to get her to see what she's doing and why. It doesn't..." Sam's voice trailed off in resignation.

"Why have we put up with it for so long?" I wondered aloud. "I'm not that masochistic, am I?"

"Dammit!" Sam exclaimed. She was seeing her own relationship with Lara coming to an end.

"I gotta move," I said again. "Don't say anything to her till I get out. Please. Give me a day or two. I'll call you."

"I'll try, but if I see her I can't just—"

"If you have to say something go ahead. Just try to give me a day or two head start." I hung up the phone and trudged home.

The next day, I did the midnight flip. With help from a couple of friends, I had my things out and in storage in three hours, all before Lara got home that night from work. I didn't have much, anyway: my bike, clothes, a few sticks of furniture that had been stored in the garage, and personal stuff like photo albums.

Part of me moved so Lara could do what she wanted. Another part of me moved because I got sick of all the bodies left in Lara's wake, especially now that I was one of them. I had been right to question her and her treatment of her lovers. And admittedly, I moved as a way of striking back at Lara, although I couldn't have imagined she cared. How could she have cared?

But leaving wasn't easy. Thoughts of Lara never left me. I had fantasized about Lara having lovers, forcing me to go down on them, or having me eat her out after she'd been with them, or at least having me watch her and her lovers in bed together. As it was I was sick and could hardly eat. Physical illness was the reality. One side of me wanted desperately to know I was the only man in her life, while the other side knew I wasn't and I hated her for it.

THAT FIRST WEEK AWAY FROM LARA WAS THE worst. I'd never been more lonely. I stayed with Loni and her boyfriend till I could get a place, then stayed at the Zen temple for a while. I avoided Lara and didn't call her. She had my number at work and could call me there if she wanted. I was sad, depressed, angry. All I hoped for was to be a little stronger each day.

About three weeks later, I ran into a woman whom I had played with at a fet party years earlier, at the liquor store where she worked. Enza was a lively, warm person in her mid twenties, and she had large brown eyes and long, silky, chestnut-coloured hair. As it happened, she and her boyfriend had just gotten a place and needed a roommate to bring down the rent. I moved in that weekend.

The place was on the third floor, up two very steep flights, above a hardware store that looked like it had stocked its shelves in 1930. The building was old and worn, and our apartment was the worst of it all. Skinheads had lived there, piling up beer cans and punching through walls. Cockroaches were everywhere. When the toilet flushed above us, water trickled through our kitchen ceiling onto the water heater in the corner.

We prepped and painted the walls, dismantled and trashed anything that looked like it had roaches, cleaned thoroughly, redid the hardwood floors and tiled the kitchen. We painted each room a different matte shade. After some hard work, the place wasn't too bad and now at least it was clean. More importantly, though, the work gave me something to think about other than Lara.

Putting Lara behind me was my greatest struggle, though, and I thought of her constantly. In my room I had photos of her and fantasized about her day and night. But I knew I was better off at a safe distance from her. I tried, instead, to channel this energy into the fet scene, which I plunged myself into once again.

Over the next few months I was out at fet

parties, slowly exploring other women, dating, still searching for something.

Angelique had frequented the Montréal scene until her employment took her to Toronto. She spoke English without an accent and was a great conversationalist. She had dirty-blonde hair and hazel eyes, an infectious laugh and a gorgeous smile. The sum of her parts was greater than the whole. I felt good around her, energized and happy—and she was quite kinky.

She loved to bind me spread-eagled and face-up on her bedroom floor, then straddle a chair over me and sit there, teasing me, taunting me incessantly for hours. She delighted in seeing me squirm and beg for relief. Then she would get off the chair and position herself over my mouth and wriggle until she got off as many times as suited her. Or she would mount me and ride me up and down, round and round, forbidding me relief while climaxing over and over. She allowed me to orgasm only when she was ready. It was incredible.

Our relationship was mostly sexual even though we got along so well. She gave me so much pure sexual satisfaction—more than any other woman had before—that I could ask for nothing more. I knew she had lots of other men but I couldn't get jealous. I accepted what she offered without complaint, which was a novelty for me.

I knew Angelique only a few months. She took my mind off Lara and what was otherwise a relatively boring time in my life. She left the scene as abruptly as she came into it, just as many fetish party patrons do.

Then there was Raffi. I met her at a fet night and tried to get her heels off but she'd had none of it. She was older than I, mid-thirties perhaps; I was about twenty-nine at the time. She was blonde as blonde can be and wore a tight-fitting black dress and fishnet stockings. She seemed straight and I figured she had likely come to the party out of curiosity. I gave her my phone number after a long conversation in which she deemed me to be more intelligent than the kind of guys she thought she'd meet there.

I didn't expect to hear from her, but she called the following week. We both worked downtown and agreed to meet for lunch. I was dressed in my usual work clothes—basic slacks, shirt, tie. Raffi, on the other hand, was more stunning that she had been at fetish night. She had on a brown designer dress-suit, sheer stockings, suede pumps to match the outfit, and wore no jewelry. She looked superb.

I was certain she would be disappointed in me, a mere minion. She was a high-roller of some sort, but somehow our conversation struck a chord and were comfortable with each other. We had chemistry if not a real sexual connection. After lunch she took me to her office on Yonge Street, a few blocks from my building.

She was a director at a large, precious-metals mining company. The foyer alone must have been 1,500 square feet; it had a massive marble desk at one end, while the other had a bank of windows that ran from floor to ceiling. We were so high up I could see the Niagara escarpment about 50 kilometers away.

"Come in," Raffi said when we reached the expanse of her private office. "Lock the door behind you."

I did.

I was nervous now and stood flatfooted in front of her desk as she swung around to her chair by the window. She had complete confidence, and why not? Her direct approach left me feeling awkward and inadequate.

"Mathew," she said, talking as if to one of her underlings, "I heard you brag the other night about your oral capabilities." She nudged her skirt a little higher. "You're going to have to put your money where your mouth is."

She looked at my pants and knew I was willing.

"But you won't be needing that," she said flatly. "You are one in a million, Mathew, and if you knew how selective I am, you'd understand. Take my word for it, and do as you're told and when, all right?"

She had a bratty, cultivated manner and it made my knees weak.

"Come here," she demanded.

I went around the desk and knelt, which pleased her.

"Closer," she instructed.

She hiked up her dress, revealing smooth, tan thighs and buttocks. She was closely shaven and taupe, just like her shoes. She draped her wonderful legs over my shoulders and held me tight and close until I was hunkered down for the long haul.

I tongued her anus, then ran up to her belly button and finished with several quick laps at her clit, then repeated this over and over. Then she instructed me to penetrate her behind with my finger. She smelled and tasted so good I didn't ever want to stop.

Her thighs squeezed me tight, making it difficult for me to breathe.

"I like a man suffocating for my orgasm," she told me.

After I was done, she handed me a towelette to clean myself, then curtly dismissed me.

Raffi wanted nothing more than my tongue and lips and got them whenever she wanted. I bargained with her and got her feet as well, time permitting. She enjoyed it thoroughly, though I could tell it would never be a passion for her. She had lovely, size six-and-a-half feet, which always smelled and tasted better than many I'd had at fetish night, especially if I got to peel her stockings off later in the day.

I knew nothing else of Raffi and never would. Our relationship continued, with varying degrees of regularity, but eventually petered out.

I felt good that I had the chance to be with these women, to explore some things that I'd missed while I was with Lara. I wasn't really engaged in Zen at this point, and I suppose I needed a distraction from the pain I felt from being away from her.

I had been on my own for about four months when I ran into Lara at a fet party. She hadn't been to one in over six months. The parties had never been a large part of her life except during the time we were together. By this time most of my resentment was gone and I was allowing myself to remember only the good things. Lara was spending a lot of time with the sam man I had found out about months earlier. When I saw her up close again, I understood my obsession with her. She was positively magnetic and radiated sexuality. Everyone around her thought they had a chance.

Lara was a little aggressive in her comments at first, which was her self-defense mechanism, but she softened after I bought her a drink. She left shortly after that, and I went about and did my thing until closing time.

I honestly don't recall how we began speaking regularly, but we did. I just couldn't resist her pull. A while later, Lara invited me out to a restaurant a few blocks down from where I lived. Dinner was on her and she ordered an expensive bottle of wine. She was relaxed but calculated. My back was to the door, and as customers came and went, a cool draft wafted across my back.

"Do you want to move, Mathew?" Lara asked. She pointed down at the floor beside her. "You'd be more comfortable here."

That was how the evening went. She pushed all my buttons with that saucy mind of hers; after all, she of all people would have known just what to say. It all led up to her asking me to move back with her. At first I didn't know what to say. To be honest, even though I was drawn to her, the prospect hadn't entered my thoughts.

"I couldn't live there with you being involved with another man," I told her, but I was happy and excited to consider being back with her—how or why I'll never really know. There was something inside me that needed closure, and deep down, that something knew it needed close proximity to her.

"That's nothing," Lara said in a comforting tone. "What you and I had was unique. I'll never have the closeness with any man that I had with you, Mathew. Never."

I was moved anytime Lara opened herself this way, because she rarely did so.

"Does he know you're thinking about having me back?"

"Yes."

"What did you tell him? That what we had was nothing, that I was just a houseboy?"

Lara just sipped her wine and swallowed the comment with it.

"I want and need you, Mathew. I love you. What we have is what we have. Nothing can be taken or needs to be added."

It sounded beautiful.

"What's the arrangement? We'll have the same problems as before. I can't stand around while you fill your bed with everyone but me." I'd told her that a million times.

"What can I say? Whatever happens happens. I'll ask for nothing from you, you ask for nothing from me."

My relationship with this woman had torn me apart, and it confounded me that I was considering moving in with her again. It was as if it was not me making a decision, but just the moment unfolding as it should, for reasons far beyond the ability of the rational mind to discern. It was all just happening.

"Let me think about it," I told her. "Give me a day or two."

The next day was Saturday. I was out all day shopping, and when I got home late in the afternoon, Lara was there talking and laughing with Enza in the kitchen.

"So, when are you moving back with Lara?" Enza asked.

I hadn't given Lara my answer yet, but she looked at me as if to say, *Yes you are, and you know it.* She was radiant and beautiful. Her toenails were French-manicured and looked magnificent. I wanted to kneel and kiss them. What was this hold she had over me?

"Whenever she says," I answered, smiling at Lara.

Lara got up and went to my room and strolled about it, inspecting me, her regained possession, approving of the pictures of her I had all about. This room had been my sanctuary, it was where I had suffered tortuous thoughts of her with that other man. Now Lara paraded through it irreverently, triumphantly, and all I wanted to do was throw myself down at her feet and beg to be used and wrung for all I was worth to her.

Moving back with Lara was a tough sell to my friends. I assured them I would not lose myself in her again, that they meant too much to me now for that. I moved my things in on my own, and at once I felt both at home and very vulnerable.

The first night home I met *him*. I imagine Lara wanted to get the inevitable out of the way. My impression had been that they were no longer intimate, but that was certainly not the case. His name was Tony. He had brought in take-out food from their favourite Italian restaurant. As we sat at the dining table, I could see that their lives were still intertwined.

He was a big man and a biker to boot, the real deal. When he had walked in the door that night, I saw him check the place out as if at any moment someone from his past, perhaps the not-too-distant past, might be waiting to attack him—not a good sign. We were polite to one another, but I could feel the tension, his dislike of my being there. I wondered how much Lara enjoyed both of us squirming just a little bit on her behalf. Tony didn't much like me despite whatever it was she had told him (that I was gay? that I meant nothing?).

After dinner I thanked them and went upstairs to straighten my room. I heard them leave later that night and didn't see Lara until she returned in the morning, wearing only her nightshirt. She had been with him, and it was as if she wanted me to know it. I could feel jealousy welling inside me worse than ever before: she'd have another man, but she wouldn't have me.

"I'm completely fucking nuts to have come back to this!" I said aloud as I watched her come through the back door.

I moved out again, as swiftly as I could, leaving the bullshit as far in the dust as possible.

THE CLOSURE I HAD NEEDED WITH LARA WAS within my grasp. When I left for the last time, my need for her, for the Mistress of my dreams, left me for good. I was purged. I felt like the luckiest person on Earth because I'd had the chance and the courage to see my fantasy through. I was reminded of something William Blake once wrote, "The road of excess leads to the palace of wisdom." The important thing was to keep walking. I knew I would never be tapping my cane on the ground, not knowing what might have been.

    I moved into a new apartment feeling like a changed, free man. I decorated it with 1930s furniture: a chaise longue, a cherry wood bar, smoking stands, floor lamps and photos and paintings from the era as well. I had friends over as soon as I was set up and had small cocktail parties before fetish parties. These gatherings were almost as fun as the parties themselves.

I was growing more connected to the world and to the things that had mattered to me besides Lara. I had several male friends, who were not from the fet world, but from my life in Zen. I saw them more often then, too. We met for ice-hockey or movies or potlucks. My meditation became more regular because of these friends, not out of anything they said, but because their lives were examples to me of what deep questioning can do. But I still had residual feelings, emotions and desires tied up in the fet scene.

My friend Edward and I began running a fetish party of our own. We approached He/She Clothing Gallery, a specialty clothing store, for sponsorship. When the store agreed to support us, we began looking for a place to hold the parties. Our objective was for our fet nights to have the benefits of both the club parties and the private ones. We wanted a more mature atmosphere, so we decided on a relatively elegant venue as opposed to the blacked-out, brick-and-concrete bars we were accustomed to. We also lowered the music level and provided plenty of equipment for players. I wanted to create an environment where people could mix and meet easily. I hoped the events would allow people to have the good fortune of living out their fantasies, so they could then make sense of them and decide for themselves which ones were important, which ones were harmful, and which ones were okay just as fantasies.

I was thirty-three and connected to the younger, less serious crowd. Edward was in his midfifties and was familiar with the older, more serious players, the active s/m community. It was a good partnership, successful in every way except financially. We never lost money, and in fact, always made a little, but never enough to justify the amount of work and grief involved in dealing with that fickle crowd. Also, our competition used its parties as a venue for advertising, had relatively unlimited funds and didn't care if they made money, all of which accounted for their longevity. Our sponsor, on the other hand, offered support through their retail outlet, but nothing in the form of money.

Our first venue was an elegant, tapestried, plushly carpeted hall in the basement of a hotel at Carlton and Jarvis streets. The room also had a small parquet dance floor, but the focus was on the play room, which we stocked with plenty of equipment: St. Andrew's crosses, benches, spreader bars, ropes, chains and all the whips and crops anyone could want.

Our next location was the former Gooderham mansion, a beautiful Victorian building on Jarvis Street. It had intricately-carved mantels, twenty-foot ceilings and a professional, formally-dressed staff. We had two parties there, distinguished by an older, mature crowd, high participation in play that went on all night, and a higher ratio of women to men, something I'd never seen at any other fet party.

Edward and I worked the room, acting as hosts, talking to people, instructing those new to erotic play. We even took part ourselves. Edward loved the parties. He loved the cross, affixing willing participants to it, where he would then work them over, slowly at first, then building strategically. He didn't care whether it was a man, woman or a transvestite on the cross. He just loved working the whip. I thought his best toy was his fish gloves, which he would don and then rub up and down his playmate. They had sandpaper palms and created a sensation somewhere between discomfort and pain when applied to the participant.

My hands, tongue and lips roamed freely, but not with the same thrill and enthusiasm of the past. I was also not afraid of offering up my posterior to the right Mistress for the night. I continued to meet and interact with all kinds of women, and I began getting offers from dominant women to serve them and to be their sub, but it just didn't feel right. A part of me wanted to jump at these chances, but another part wanted nothing of it.

One Mistress who almost got me was Shelly, a petite brunette with short, dark hair and blue eyes. She had that sleeper librarian look on the surface; but underneath she had sexy, muscular thighs and calves and outstanding feet, which she took great care in keeping soft and supple. As I feared, while she was allowing me to live out one of my life-long fantasies, it came off as dry and unexciting. I was too aware of the fantasies at play; the moment we shared became one of hyper-awareness rather than of fantasy. I was still fresh from being with Lara and the idea of anything serious with any woman gave me the creeps. Certainly a Mistress/slave relationship made no sense to me anymore. I don't believe a woman will continue to respect a subservient man. Most sub men want an actual relationship with a dom, whereas dom women will have their slave and want a regular relationship with someone else. That man will take priority over the sub.

Shelly also liked variety. I knew I wasn't the only sub in her life, another issue I'd encountered with many dom women in the past. I knew that if I was going to devote myself to anyone ever again, I wanted that same devotion returned, however it was manifested. It wasn't long before I drifted away from Shelly. It simply became clear that there was a need in me more important than any relationship I could engineer.

    Another venue for the parties was the rear bar and deck of a former cruise ship that was permanently docked in Toronto's harbour. We filled the deck with equipment rented from a movie-prop warehouse, staying with the nautical theme. There was a crow's nest for caging people, a plank to bind people to and yards and yards of rope. We dubbed the party DAS *stiletto* BOOT, and it took place on a hot, late-August evening. Everybody played that night. The best moment was when two gorgeous women, one blonde, the other brunette, both dressed from top to bottom in white PVC, showed up in a shiny, white convertible Porsche 911, and took over the party for an hour or two. They took one sub and wrapped him head to toe in industrial-strength plastic wrap and bound him to a pillar. Then they took turns whipping him, as they only had one cat-o-nine tails. They ended it with a long sensual kiss in front of their blissful victim. Then they left, as abruptly as they came.

Our finest location was a relatively small second floor studio above a vintage furniture store on Queen Street East known as the Volcano Room. The proprietors had furnished it in 1950s parephernalia—sofa's, lamps, tables, ashtrays, you name it. There was a small stream and waterfall leading down to a separate room, where we had our dungeon. This venue was excellent because it was true to the private party atmosphere, and the party lasted until six in the morning. Edward and I did everything. It was BYOB so that made it simpler for us. There was no air conditioning, which made it stiflingly hot, but somehow it seemed appropriate. The partygoers got down and dirty, and took liberties they wouldn't have taken in a club. It was more of a sex party. We got complaints from the older, more mature crowd we had been catering to because they thought this kind of event could draw negative attention, even from the police.

There were other locations, too. We were always looking for our own spot, our own little private s/m parlour. Unfortunately rents were too high, and the numbers didn't add up. The fet community is a small one. Going out completely on our own seemed a big risk, especially when I had grave doubts that I would remain in the scene at all. It was becoming difficult for me to participate as each new party came and went. I found that even though the parties were fun and successful, my heart wasn't really in it. The fet scene had been a part of my life, perhaps my whole life, for so long. Now it was like I was struggling to find a new place in the scene by throwing the parties. Nothing I tried sparked a fire in me. I was hanging on out of pure habit.

Edward and I ground the parties to a halt. I had not gone to any of the other parties for months. I had had a shift in imagination. As much as I participated in the scene and sought companionship, there was emptiness to it all. My reality had no more substance than my fantasy.

    Everything I tried to possess was on fire: there was no one, nothing I could hold on to. I had tried to lose myself in Zen and then to find myself by indulging in my fetish, both without success. I thought seriously for the first time in eleven years about leaving the city and the scene that had become my home. I had close friends—a few that stood by me from Zen, a few from the fetish scene—but they had their lives, jobs and families and weren't enough to keep me in Toronto. There was nothing tying me to the city. All I had was my natural koans: *What am I? What is this?* Now they were not so much burning a hole in me as they were naturally sinking deep. I didn't even have to ask the questions anymore because they asked themselves. Everything around me was becoming these questions.

My work, too, was dragging me down. I was not meant for the corporate grind, let alone banking. So I accepted a layoff, severance and half of my pension contributions, and tried to restructure my life so that I could approach the questions recurring in my consciousness with vigour.

I bought a camper van, sold everything and began cultivating a relationship with nature with my friend Sean from the Zen centre. We began camping and body surfing on the Great Lakes, at places like Presqu'isle, Rock Point and Wasaga Beach. Slowly I began to see the kind of life I needed to live. Sean had camped on the west coast of Vancouver Island and had seen surfing there. He told me, "Man, if you're sick of the city and want to surf, take your camper and go."

A few farewell parties later and I was

gone. I took my koan to the old-growth forest and the open ocean on the West Coast, and surrounded myself with their power.

    I moved to a patch of rain forest with 700-year-old cedars and towering hemlocks, with salal, salmonberry and devil's club competing with me for space. There, in that sun-dappled, salt-sea air, among bears, wolves, whales and sea lions, I began to see.

BOTH FETISH AND ZEN, TWO SEEMINGLY STRANGE bedfellows, supported each other throughout my spiritual search. Zen provided the means for my questioning, fetish provided the inspiration with which to glimpse into the nature of thought and desire—it was the fuel for my questioning.

By this time I had confronted and experienced all my desires and fantasies to the fullest extent. I had done all I could in the physical world and with the rational mind. It was time to let go and allow my questioning to sink even deeper, time to let it encompass everything I smelled, saw, felt, tasted and heard. During my years in Zen I had never surrendered myself like this on the sitting mat. My practice had been insincere and forced.

There is an ancient mystic symbol, the endless knot, which I feel embodies my mystic experience. It is a symbol that represents many things to many cultures. It can be found in the Celtic culture; at the centre of the famous paradox of the Gordian knot; and it is also one of the eight symbols represented on the Buddha, just to name a few examples. It is a symbol that has come to represent a myriad of concepts, from the concrete to the ethereal—the surge of waves; attachment; bondage; paradox, resolution and liberation; perpetual motion; infinity; the endless cycle of rebirth; the Oneness and interconnectedness of the universe. For me, the endless knot represents a belief that the universe is infinitely interconnected, with no beginning and no end, and that we are this Oneness.

 I believe that everything contained within this Oneness is in perpetual motion, and therefore, nothing is ever permanent. For example, consider the cycle of thought-desire-action-memory, where thought spurs desire, which creates an impulse to act; the action is imprinted on the mind as memory, which in turn sparks thought, and so on. In the past, I wanted to cling to one thought, desire, action or memory and claim it as my identity. It was my struggle to find permanence within constant change that made me feel trapped.

As I allowed my questions *What am I? What is this?* to sink deeper, I was able to move past thought to what lies beyond. Going past thought to what lies beyond means letting thoughts and feelings alone without clinging to them, without drawing them out of the natural flow of thoughts and feelings, without getting caught up in their resultant dramas. In this way, I began to see my thoughts and feelings rather than trying to control them or impulsively act on them. I watched them rather than getting lost in them. This shift in perspective allowed me to see that the thoughts, feelings and desires that I felt had enslaved me since childhood were not me, and that they are ever changing. Once I thought I was a child, then I thought I was a student, then an adult, a Zen practitioner, a fetishist, a slave, someone with answers. Someday I'll be a senior and eventually I'll be dead. But am I any of those things? What am I really?

In the past, everything I desired—fetish party after fetish party, woman after woman, one pair of feet after another—came and went. These lustful needs continued unabated until I saw in their impermanence that they were simply a result of my mind clinging to my ephemeral thoughts, fantasies and longings. I realized all of these desires, thoughts and actions pass by what we really are—our true nature remains throughout, whole and complete, lacking nothing. What could possibly exist outside of myself—money, sex, fetish, relationships, jobs—that could make me whole?

My answer came as a result of immersing myself in the moment, simply observing my mind and body and present feelings, sensations, thoughts, desires, and not attaching myself to them. We can do this anywhere—an office, a classroom, a sex party, a surfboard. For me it was once at fetish parties, now it is in nature. Surfing has become integral to my connection with nature. I feel truly immersed in the moment while riding waves. Waves embody the very nature of the universe, emerging out of a vastness, existing, folding back in again. There is little room for idle thinking with a ten-foot wall of water bearing down upon you and your board. As a result, surfing affords me clarity.

My experiences have not eliminated my sexual interests from my life. Instead, I try to cultivate an unclinging mind so each moment will unfold without my manipulations, unfolding as it should. I no longer have a fetish, nor a need to submit to a woman in any way. However, I have many friends in the scene, and still go to the odd fet party. The difference is that now, when any fetish-related fantasies come up, I am able to let go of them. Sometimes I try to remember what it was I felt then, when I was involved in the fet scene, because I can look at a pair of feet now and wonder what it was that I saw in them.

Of course, there are still aspects of my previous involvement with fetish that come up from time to time, but in a totally different context. If these issues come up when I am with a woman with whom I can communicate with and trust, I am able to express that side of myself fully.

My awareness has shown me that in the end it is simple: all but what we really are changes ceaselessly. Clinging to this ceaseless change or trying to control it causes suffering. Through insight and awareness we can learn to be with the moment, without attachment. We can see freedom in the endless knot of existence.

A woman works her strong hands over my body, kneading knots borne of yet another one of my surf sessions. She circulates her hands and thus my blood. I am rejuvenated. She rolls me onto my back and mounts me. She has her way, slowly rocking and rotating herself on top of me. I hold her sides just below her breasts and feel the breath of this creature—in, out, in, out.

When she is through with me, it is my turn. As she lies, exhausted, I begin by kissing her hands, which have brought me so much pleasure, and then move to her face, her happy, kissable face. From there it is down, around, up and under, overlooking nothing. I smell, lick and nibble at her feet, her soft soles, her round toes, taking each one in my mouth and sucking hard, massaging their bottoms with my tongue, not because I'd planned to, but because I feel it in the moment.

She writhes in orgasm, and I kiss her more passionately. I can't help myself. Soon I am on top and inside her again, and as I move, she undulates, wavelike, emerging out of a vastness, being, folding back in again...